When Churches Mind the Children

The High/Scope Press
High/Scope Educational Research Foundation

When Churches Mind the Children

A Study of Day Care in Local Parishes

Eileen W. Lindner
Mary C. Mattis
June R. Rogers

with contributions by
James T. Bond

with commentary by
Peggy L. Shriver, National Council of Churches
Gwen G. Morgan, Wheelock College

sponsored by the
National Council of Churches

THE HIGH/SCOPE PRESS

Published by
THE HIGH/SCOPE PRESS
High/Scope Educational Research Foundation
600 North River Street
Ypsilanti, Michigan 48197
(313) 485-2000

Library of Congress Cataloging in Publication Data

Lindner, Eileen W., 1949–
When churches mind the children.

Includes bibliographical references. 1. Day Care centers—United States—Case studies. 2. Church and education—United States—Case studies. 3. National Council of the Churches of Christ in the United States of America. I. Mattis, Mary C. II. Rogers, June R. III. Title.

HV854.L54 1983 362.7′12′0973 83-22545

ISBN 0-931114-23-3

Printed in the United States of America

To those who provide child care in our nation's churches, in the hope that our work will encourage a greater appreciation of yours.

Contents

Acknowledgments

Some readers would consider it great folly to survey nearly 100,000 parishes about their weekday programs serving children. Both the Church and child day care have well-earned reputations as enigmas, and only the most foolhardy would try to study them at the same time. Despite the complex, confusing, and chaotic demands inherent in such a work, our burden as authors of the present study was greatly reduced by the willingness of many to shoulder a portion of the load throughout the development of the Child Day Care Project of the National Council of the Churches of Christ in the United States of America.

We owe a profound debt, of course, to the 15 communions that, motivated by a deep concern for young children, initiated the Project and made possible such an extensive ecumenical study. Meeting together as the Child Advocacy Working Group, the following representatives of national church agencies have given shape, direction, and purpose to our work and will be the direct recipients of its outcome: American Baptist Churches—Reverend Leonard Wilmot; American Lutheran Church—Sandra Holloway; Christian Church (Disciples of Christ)—Reverend Rolland Pfile; The Episcopal Church—Woodrow S. Carter, Sr.; Greek Orthodox Archdiocese of North and South America—Elaine Gounaris; Lutheran Church in America—Audrey Russell; Presbyterian Church in the United States—Frances Johns; United Church of Christ—Lois Peeler, Helen Webber; United Methodist Church—Barbara Garcia, Lucy Gist, Beverly Jackson, Mary Jane Pierce Norton, Bonnie Offrink, Linda Schulze, June Shimokawa, Chiquita Smith, and Bertha Swindall; United Presbyterian Church in the United States of America—Roxanne Coop.

Kenyon Burke, Associate General Secretary, Division of Church and Society, National Council of the Churches of Christ, U.S.A., provided guidance when asked, and moral support without being asked, throughout the Project. Colleagues within the Division of Church and Society bore the inconvenience of tens of thousands of questionnaires with good cheer and much encouragement. All deserve our thanks.

We wish to thank Carnegie Corporation of New York, which provided financial support for the Project. To Barbara Finberg, Vice President, Program, we owe a long-standing debt for her generous gifts of patience and insight. Gloria Brown, Program Associate, raised many thoughtful questions and was unfailing in her optimism. Carnegie Corporation is, of course, not responsible for statements or views expressed in this report.

Likewise we want to thank the Foundation for Child Development and the Ford Foundation, both of which provided support for regional conferences of church-related providers through which additional perspectives on church-housed child care were gained. These foundations, of course, are not responsible for the statements or views expressed herein. Jane Dustan, Vice-President of the Foundation for Child Development, has consistently been a wise contributor to the shape and design of the project. Prudence Brown, Program Officer of the Ford Foundation, too, contributed thoughtful questions that saved us more than once from errors.

We are grateful to the Reverend Robert Rodisch, General Director of the Support Agency, United Presbyterian Church in the United States of America, who in an ecumenical spirit made available Mary C. Mattis to serve as the Research Consultant to the Project. Ann Bright of the same agency was unflappable through many revisions of the instruments and earns our thanks.

Our thanks include, too, Louis Maday, Teachers' College, Columbia University, who tirelessly carried the computer responsibilities of the Project.

Many colleagues in church agencies, child advocacy organizations, day care centers, and universities spent long hours helping us plan the study, refine the questionnaires, and later make sense of the responses. While we will not risk listing them and possibly omitting one or two, we want to express our thanks to them.

We owe a special thanks to the thousands of pastors and directors of child care programs who completed our questionnaires and shared with us much surprising and sometimes poignant information about their work with young children. The hundreds who expressed delight in our efforts and wrote us messages of cheer hold a special place in our minds.

As we moved toward the preparation of this report, Dana Friedman became our colleague and friend. Her vast knowledge and diligence in tracking down details renewed our own pursuit.

James T. Bond, Director of Research, High/Scope Educational Research Foundation, who served as our consultant, brought an uncommon kindness and thoroughness to our work. In thanking him we must acknowledge especially his willingness and even eagerness to understand the complexities of American church life. On numerous occasions, and particularly in the preparation of Chapter III, we depended on his wisdom and insight and were not once disappointed. Throughout our long efforts his concern and interest relieved the preparation of this report from tedium.

Our gratitude includes a special thanks to Gwen Morgan, Child Care Consultant and Lecturer, Wheelock College, and Peggy Shriver, Associate General Secretary, Office of Research, Evaluation, and Planning, National Council of the Churches of Christ, U.S.A., for their fine commentaries.

Paul F. Goodman, Project Assistant to the Child Day Care Project, saw us and the task through from its earliest stages to publication. His many contributions and his versatility in meeting the challenges that arose continuously earn him both our thanks and our deep respect.

Though everyone mentioned has contributed far beyond our ability to repay, we want to acknowledge their efforts and extend our most profound thanks. Additionally we want to relieve them of responsibility for the opinions ventured herein, for those are exclusively the province of the authors and represent neither the National Council of the Churches of Christ, U.S.A., nor the Child Advocacy Working Group. Likewise, the errors that have stubbornly lingered in the text are also the responsibility of the authors.

Rev. Eileen W. Lindner, Director
Child Advocacy Office
National Council of Churches

June R. Rogers, Associate Director
Child Advocacy Office
National Council of Churches

Mary C. Mattis, Research Consultant
Child Day Care Project

When Churches Mind the Children

I
Prologue

A much loved hymn of the Church instructs the faithful that "new occasions teach new duties" and that "time makes ancient good uncouth." The history of American churches and their ministries to children reflects this striving to meet new occasions with new programs and initiatives. Historically, much, though by no means all, of the work of churches with children has focused on education. During the nation's colonial period and through the early years of the republic, churches were major providers of and advocates for children's education. By teaching the reading of the Psalter and by founding schools and academies, churches expressed their deep concern for the intellectual and spiritual well-being of children.

In periods of war and economic hardship, the Church has carried out ministries of benevolence with children and their families. Acting out of a sense of love of neighbor, the Church has frequently offered direct financial aid and provided food, clothing, and shelter to the widows and orphans of war. Through foundling hospitals and orphanages, the Church has sometimes assumed custody for children whose parents could not or would not provide for them.

Faced with a great swell in immigration late in the 19th century, the churches—Protestant and Catholic—established many aid societies, settlement houses, and recreational programs for children who had been immersed abruptly in an alien culture and urban poverty. Historical commitments to both education and spiritual well-being shaped many of the church efforts of the period. Moreover, the human consequences of urbanization and industrialization, as well as immigration, taught new duties. Preceding and during the Progressive Era, American Christianity experienced what it has come to call the Social Gospel. This outcropping of social witness taught new approaches and applications of the developing social sciences. Regarding children, new insights prompted programs geared to ideas of child development and the child's need for healthful recreation as well as adequate sanitation and nutrition. In this era, day nurseries in church-sponsored settlement and neighborhood houses explicitly provided children with learning opportunities, in addition to ensuring supervision in a clean and safe environment.

Early in the 20th century, the reforming climate within many American churches provided support and leadership to the long campaign for the abolition of child labor. Advocacy for children and their needs was to become a lasting feature of the cooperative efforts of the churches. Direct services to children in the areas of education, spiritual training, recreation, health, and nutrition persisted throughout two World Wars and into the present period. Also, advocacy for public policies responsive to the needs of children became part of the churches' ministries.

In each age, however, individual churches developed their own patterns of response to children's needs. Informed by their various theological perspectives as well as by different social and cultural backgrounds, the denominations sought various paths to faithfulness, each denomination choosing its own way of expressing its vocation or ministry to children and families. Many churches began to ally themselves through ecumenical agencies to give expression to their common social ministry as well as to their Christian unity.

Today churches continue to perceive different needs among children and families and to respond to these needs in different ways. Some—guided by their theology, history, and tradition—have confined their ministry with children to the areas of religious education and family programs. Often characterized by a dogged defense of traditional family patterns based upon a particular understanding of biblical literature, these churches seek through their ministries to restore families. It is their conviction that the only way to meet the needs of children is to enable their parents to conform with what is perceived to be the biblical ideal of family structure and life.

Other churches, believing that families are best supported through just and sensitive public policy, extend the scope of their ministry. In addition to religious education and family programs, many of these churches actively engage in child advocacy informed by biblical and theological understandings of the concepts of love and justice. Drawn together in a common sense of gospel imperative and vocation, some of these churches work ecumenically through the National Council of the Churches of Christ, U.S.A.

National Council of Churches

A coalition of 32 denominations or communions, the National Council of Churches (NCC) was founded in 1950 to carry out the programs of several early ecumenical agencies that preceded it. Comprising various "mainline Protestant" denominations as well as Anglican and Orthodox churches, the NCC has contact with some 41 million American Christians. Governed by representatives of member churches, the NCC strives to express Christian unity through a variety of activities including publication of educational materials, international and national relief work, production of materials and programs for use in local parishes, research on issues of religious significance, and diverse programs designed to alleviate human suffering. By creating a common forum for Christian mission and social witness, the NCC provides churches with a means for undertaking programs that exceed the resources of any single church.

As a part of its social witness, the NCC often issues public declarations on current national and international issues. By such policy statements, the NCC has brought theological reflection to those concerns that command the attention of thoughtful citizens in the United States. Basing its actions upon its policy statements, the NCC has frequently acted as an advocate for justice for all persons and for the adoption of practices that would enable the fullest measure of life to those without means, prestige, or power.

The various program units of the NCC maintain a wide range of relationships with church agencies throughout the United States. Through state and local councils of churches as well as through regional structures of member churches, the NCC has access to an infrastructure perhaps second only to that of public education. With its ability to contact clergy persons and networks of Christians concerned about specific issues such as hunger or peace and nuclear disarmament, the NCC can reach deep into American life. Because it maintains regular contact with many parishes, the NCC is strengthened in its efforts by being well informed about the specific needs and problems of local communities.

While the NCC maintains and promotes dialogue among Christians, it recognizes that many persons within and without the Church disagree from time to time with NCC programs or public stances. Member denominations or communions differ widely in the ways and the extent to which they keep their local parishes informed of the work of the NCC. Some local parishes are largely unaware of the programs of the NCC, while others regularly draw upon its resources.

Not all of America's Christians are represented in the NCC structures. Indeed, several major Christian churches, for example the Southern Baptist Convention and the Roman Catholic Church, are not members. Many other churches are independent, local entities that have no national structure and thus cannot be systematically included in the leadership of the Council. However, many non-member churches do participate in selected NCC programs. And as the largest ecumenical agency in the nation, the National Council of Churches represents a broad segment of American religious life.

Child Advocacy as Ministry

Like many of its member churches, the NCC has a long history of work for children. Often carried out by offices of the Ministry with Children, this work has been devoted largely to educational goals, such as development of the widely used uniform Sunday school curriculum. Other work has been dedicated to children with some special need, such as those who have mental or physical disabilities or who are housed in institutions.

Once again, recognizing that new occasions were requiring of them new duties, a number of member churches requested assistance from the NCC in reconsidering their approaches to problems confronting children in this country. In the autumn of 1977, the Working Group on Justice for Children and Youth (subsequently renamed the Child Advocacy Working Group) was established as a program area within the Division of Church and Society of the National Council of Churches. In the course of identifying and examining a broad range of problems affecting children and their families, the Group soon came to focus on pressures external to the family that affect all its members and over which individual families have little or no control. This, in turn, led to concern with society's obligation to the child, especially as expressed through public policy.

In July of 1978, the Working Group established the Child and Family Justice Project, which was intended to collect firsthand information about the problems affecting American families and to consider the relationships between these problems and current public policies. During the next two and one-half years, the Project operated in 20 locations throughout the nation. The Child and Family Justice Project challenged the Church to consider public policy approaches to the needs of children and their families. The Project was explicit in its assumption that effective child advocacy would require structural changes in the socioeconomic system, aided by the implementation of new public policies, in addition to more traditional programs providing direct services to individual children and families.

The social analysis conducted in the 20 community locations of the Project provided extensive information about specific factors affecting children and families. Of these the single most pervasive and pressing family concern identified by the Child and Family Justice Project was access to child day care.

Within its own life, the Church had a curious relation to the provision of child care. Local parishes had responded to child day care needs in quite different ways, each according to its own perception of the need and of its responsibility and capacity to respond. No data were then available to provide a coherent picture of the extent or nature of church involvement in the provision of child care. No national church agency even recorded the names or numbers of parishes operating child day care centers.

Child Day Care as an Issue

Having identified child day care as a central concern of American families, the Child Advocacy Working Group sought further understanding of the issue to guide policy formulation and program development. The Group was soon confronted by a bewildering array of information and misinformation. Most significant was the seeming inability of any agency to describe accurately the dimensions of child day care. Neither private research efforts nor government records provided accurate and up-to-date estimates of the number of day care programs or providers, or of the number of children in day care in the United States.

Although inconclusive with regard to the number of children cared for, available evidence did point to several factors that were likely to increase the demand for day care over the coming years. Out of economic necessity and/or personal desire, the number of women entering and remaining in the labor force was growing. As of March 1980, 43% of all children under six years of age had mothers in the labor force.[1] Moreover, it was estimated that about 11 million more women would enter the labor force in the next decade.[2] One obvious factor motivating more and more women to work was an escalating divorce rate, and single parents who work require day care for their young children. In addition, many couples were choosing to delay childbirth until their 30s, at which point women often have well-established careers that they are reluctant to leave. Also, trends toward smaller families diminished the possibility that other siblings could care for preschoolers. Lastly, parents of young children were increasingly unable to call upon members of their extended families for child care support because of residential mobility and changing values.

There seemed little reason to doubt that the demand for day care would grow substantially over the next decade. But what of the supply?

---

[1] Personick, V. A. The outlook for industry output and employment through 1990. *Monthly Labor Review*, August 1981, **104**(8), 29.

[2] U.S. Department of Labor, Bureau of Labor Statistics. *Handbook of labor statistics*, 1980, Table 59.

Already many families faced a profound dilemma. On the one hand, in order to work parents were forced to place their young children in some form of day care. On the other hand, many were not able to find fully satisfactory care that they could afford. Who were the providers of child day care in these communities? How would they cope with the growing demand for services when they seemed unable to meet current needs? What was, and might be, the role of the Church in child day care provision?

Obtaining child day care services in the United States has always been and remains the responsibility of individual families. In contrast to governmental guarantees of education and health care for all citizens, government has not assumed responsibility for providing or ensuring universal access to child day care. Although government has made some contribution by subsidizing services to selected low-income families and by offering nonrefundable tax credits for child care expenses to all taxpayers, it has not assumed the major burden. Indeed, government has done rather little to systematically shape the development of child day care services. Efforts at regulation to ensure health, safety, and quality have been sporadic and inconsistent. Inconsistent regulation, together with unstable governmental subsidies, has tended to increase uncertainty and concern among providers and clients. Current consideration by government of replacing direct subsidies for eligible providers with vouchers given directly to low-income parents is introducing new uncertainties into the day care market.

Although available information did not provide the Child and Family Justice Project with a detailed picture of the child care industry in the 20 communities studied, much less in the nation as a whole, it was apparent that the service system was diverse and fragmented. The major costs of care were borne not by government but by individual families and even by the providers themselves, who often "subsidize" programs by accepting low wages and making various non-cash contributions. The major source of services was not public but private—individual providers operating out of their own homes, non-profit organizations, small proprietorships, some commercial firms, and churches. Perhaps the most salient feature of the industry was its lack of organization, which made any sort of coordinated planning, advocacy, lobbying, or investment impossible and which made it extraordinarily difficult to obtain even the most basic information about who was served, in what ways, and at what cost.

The Child Advocacy Working Group concluded that such disarray in the child care industry was likely to put children and families at increasing risk as demand outstripped the supply of affordable, quality care. It seemed imperative that both local and national discussions of child day care needs and policies be initiated to ameliorate current problems and to avoid even more serious deficiencies in service. Crucial to any dialogue at the local or national level would be the voice of child day care providers, a largely unorganized and unidentified constituency. Without their involvement, it would be impossible to formulate viable strategies for meeting the growing child care needs of American families.

The Child Day Care Project

In 1980, after careful consideration of the issues related to day care, the Child Advocacy Working Group established the Child Day Care Project within the Child Advocacy Office of the NCC. The Group recognized that many church buildings serve as locations for child care centers and that the church potentially had access to large numbers of providers. Although no denomination kept systematic records on the child day care programs operating in its parishes, all denominations maintained mailing lists that provided direct access to pastors. It was somewhat startling to realize that these mailing lists might contain the addresses of more child day care providers than any other lists ever assembled.

As a first step in addressing the national day care dilemma, staff of the Child Day Care Project, with a grant from Carnegie Corporation of New York, undertook what may be the most extensive survey of child day care in the nation's history. At the outset of the research phase of the Project, we attempted to clarify our own assumptions and aspirations. In undertaking such an ambitious study, we had to be certain that it would not claim too much for itself. The study is not an exercise in state-of-the-art research design, although considerable effort was made to employ sound methodology. Rather, the study is best understood as an initial attempt to map uncharted territory. As such it draws not a detailed portrait but a profile of church-housed child care and raises as many questions as it answers.

The study was explicitly intended, not to be an apologetic for the Church, but to uncover as much information as possible about the nature of child day care programs operating in church buildings. In preparing to undertake this study, many secular as well as church persons were consulted. During this process, some fears and doubts were expressed about the quality and openness of church-housed programs. Variously it was believed that the Church offers only part-day nursery school, is frequently the "slumlord" for child care, often restricts enrollment to children of church members, and resists enrolling publicly subsidized children in its programs. We were prepared to confirm these beliefs if true, but all these generalizations proved far too sweeping. The picture that emerged of church-housed child care was far more diverse in every way than anyone had imagined. While it is possible that churches housing programs of the sort suggested above simply failed to respond to the questionnaires they received, the very substantial number of programs that did respond defies such facile explanation.

The ultimate purpose of the Child Day Care Project is not research but action informed by research and by the various stakeholders in child day care. In designing and carrying out the study, we took great care not to allow the research to be colored by preconceived notions of what actions ought to be taken. The Child Advocacy Working Group undertook the Project without any preconceived policy stance other than a commitment to support quality child care.

It should also be pointed out that, by focusing the research on church-housed programs, the Child Advocacy Working Group did not intend to treat church-housed child care in isolation from the larger child care market. Rather, the Project was specifically intended to bring church-housed programs into closer relationship with the issues, advocacy, and constituency of "secular" child day care, and toward that end initial plans included the development of an Ecumenical Child Care Network. It is hoped that current efforts to build this network will bring the Church into the ongoing national dialogue and perhaps make some contribution to that dialogue. The research activities of the Project can be viewed as an initial outreach to an unorganized voice in the child care community, one that happens to reside in the nation's churches.

The three chapters that follow report the information gleaned from two questionnaires, numerous follow-up telephone interviews, and site visits by Project staff. The Epilogue considers the implications of this information for action.

II
Stained Glass Windows on Child Care: The Church as Provider

The title for this chapter was not selected merely as a playful variation on the title of an earlier study of day care—*Windows on Day Care*[3]— but also as one that captured something of our experience as we tried to peer in upon child care in our nation's churches. The very character of the Church altered what we saw, as though the window we looked through was of stained glass. For good or for ill— and that will be a subject of much debate—the Church frequently offers more than space to the child care programs that operate within its buildings. It, like a multicolored stained glass window, splashes color and meaning, sometimes capriciously, sometimes quite intentionally, upon those who dwell within.

The Child Day Care Project's study of church-housed child care was restricted to the parishes of 15 of the National Council of Churches' member denominations or communions that elected to participate in the research. A necessary first step in learning more about the nature and extent of church-housed programs was to identify existing programs through a census of all parishes of the participating denominations. In February of 1982, a brief questionnaire was mailed to the pastors of 87,562 churches. It was designed to identify the general types of programs available, if any; the relationships of programs to congregations; the types of communities in which parishes were located; and, most important for the continuing work of the Project, the names of child day care program directors. For purposes of the Project, "child day care" was defined as any program providing nonresidential care for children from birth through elementary school, including before- and after-school care but excluding school programs for children of school age. The initial questionnaire is reproduced in Appendix 1.

By the April 1982 cut-off date, 25,069 parishes had responded to the initial questionnaire, representing an overall response rate of nearly 29%,

---

[3]Keyserling, M. D. *Windows on day care*. New York: National Council of Jewish Women, 1972.

which was higher than expected. Of these respondents, about one third (8,767) reported that some sort of child day care was provided on church premises. Since many churches housed more than one type of program, the total number of programs indicated (14,589) far exceeded the number of parishes reporting provision of day care. (These basic statistics are presented by denomination in Table 1.) Whether the proportion of churches housing child day care is the same among parishes that did not respond to the initial questionnaire is not known. Nevertheless, the 8,767 parishes that reported housing some sort of child day care program, and the 14,589 programs offered, represent very large numbers by any standard and suggest that church-housed programs probably constitute the largest group of day care providers in the nation.

It is worth noting in this context that the 15 participating denominations listed in Table 1 are not representative of all denominations in the nation, and therefore the findings of this study should not be generalized to nonparticipating denominations. Moreover, the findings reported here should be generalized to participating denominations only with some qualification, since only 29% of parishes responded to the initial questionnaire.

Although the participating denominations vary considerably among themselves with respect to size, geographical distribution, types of communities in which parishes are located, and sociocultural characteristics of their congregations, the study sample does disproportionately represent churches located in suburbs and small cities or towns of the Midwest—churches serving mainly white, middle-class congregations. The complexion of the study sample simply reflects the dominant pattern among participating denominations. The research design employed in the study does not permit inferences about possible variations in the incidence of church-housed programs by denomination, region, or community type.

In addition to returning the questionnaire, hundreds of respondents also wrote letters or enclosed materials descriptive of the programs housed in their churches. This unsolicited information suggested just how complex the study of church-housed child care would be. The rich variety of program types and sponsorship arrangements respondents described sorely tested working definitions of child day care "program" and "provider" but began to provide the fuller perspective on day care that the Child Advocacy Working Group was seeking.

This chapter addresses a series of rather general questions intended to provide a backdrop for the more detailed statistical findings from the follow-up survey discussed in the next chapter. The first question has already been considered:

- How prevalent is church-housed child day care?

Table 1

Number of Parishes Involved in the Initial Survey by Denomination

Denomination	Number of Questionnaires Mailed	Number of Responses by Deadline†	Number of Parishes Reporting Some Program	Number of Programs Reported
African Methodist Episcopal	2,125	•	19	51
African Methodist Episcopal Zion	1,291	•	11	24
American Baptist Churches in the U.S.A.	5,844	•	523	859
American Lutheran Church	400	•	249	416
Christian Church (Disciples)	4,587	•	365	624
Christian Methodist Episcopal Church	2,109	•	21	38
Episcopal Church	7,572	•	877	1,379
Greek Orthodox Archidiocese of North and South America	462	•	17	23
Lutheran Church in America	5,412	•	578	905
Presbyterian Church in the U.S.	2,825	•	652	1,193
Progressive National Baptist Convention in the U.S.	1,006	•	36	82
Reformed Church in America	2,500	•	98	163
United Church of Christ	4,840	•	813	1,274
United Methodist Church	37,628	•	2,958	5,067
United Presbyterian Church in the U.S.A.	8,961	•	1,463	2,352
Other or unclassifiable	—	•	87	139
Totals	87,562	25,069	8,767	14,589

†Responses that did not indicate that some child day care program was housed in the church were not tallied by denomination.

The answer: very prevalent. On the following pages, a number of other questions are addressed in some detail:

- How are churches involved in the provision of child care?
- Why is the Church involved in child care?
- How have local parishes become involved in child care?

Although exhaustive and definitive answers are not possible, cautious analysis suggests tentative answers that may provoke and inform further discussion of the central issues.

While statistical information from the questionnaires is useful for characterizing church-housed child care as a whole, it cannot portray individual programs as integrated, human systems responding over time to changing conditions. Thus in this chapter, we present more complete portraits of individual programs by supplementing the statistical data with information drawn from the letters and materials that accompanied many questionnaires. Information about selected programs has also been obtained from follow-up telephone interviews and actual visits to programs chosen in a random fashion from those responding. Using information from this study and elsewhere, we have also tried to draw a portrait of the Church as a religious, social, and economic setting for child care.

Detailed statistical analyses of the objectives, practices, staffing patterns, administrative arrangements, and economics of church-housed programs appear in the next chapter. There, information from a lengthy follow-up questionnaire is presented for the total sample of respondents and for several sub-sample comparisons: church-operated versus independently operated centers, for-profit versus non-profit centers, and part-time versus full-time preschool programs.

How Are Churches Involved in the Provision of Child Care?

When viewed from the local level, the issues surrounding church involvement in child care are rather different than when viewed from the national level.

Local Involvement

The initial questionnaire asked pastors to indicate, for each program mentioned, whether the church operated the program or simply provided space for program operations. Responses to this question revealed that 53% of all programs mentioned are, in the judgment of pastors, operated by the parish itself, while 47% are independently operated on church premises. These findings, together with the large number of programs involved, leave no doubt that the Church is a major *direct* provider of child day care in the United States.

It is also apparent from the sheer number of programs housed on church property, but not operated by the parishes, that the Church plays a significant *indirect* role in the provision of child day care as evidently the largest single landlord for day care programs in the nation. In addition, information from the follow-up survey, reported in the next chapter, reveals that frequently churches are benevolent landlords, charging nothing or less than fair market value for the use of property and various essential services. Thus, even when parishes do not operate the programs housed on their premises, they often make substantial contributions and might legitimately be considered *co-providers* of care.

While many local parishes provide child care in varying degrees, their efforts have not been formally organized into a child care *delivery system*. Despite the highly organized nature of most American denominations, little of that organization is apparent in the child care programs sponsored by local parishes. Indeed, it was an awareness of this lack of organization, intentionality, and information that provided some of the initiative for the Child Day Care Project.

National Involvement

National church agencies have not exercised much control or direction of church-housed child care programs. For example, no national organization or headquarters of a church, prior to the Child Day Care Project, kept records of which local parishes were providing child care. Perhaps even more surprising is the total absence of guidelines and recommendations for child care provision emanating from church hierarchies. Notable tractarians, the bureaucracies of the churches make available to their parishes a veritable blizzard of "how to" books regarding such diverse subjects as evangelism, fund-raising for pipe organs or stained glass windows, and organization of church fairs. The absence of specific guidance for developing or operating child care programs stands in sharp contrast to the national guidance offered in other areas of social justice and social ministry carried out by local parishes.

Likewise, in the area of personnel, the official posture has largely been one of indifference. While there are associations of church workers, denominational caucuses of church secretaries, and very formal credentialing patterns and associations for religious educators, no attempts have been made by national church agencies to organize church-related child day care providers. In most instances, child care directors, teachers, and aides are not, in fact, employees of the congregation. But, even in cases where the child care staff serves a program wholly operated by the congregation, staff members are not considered to be church employees in the same sense that clergy, secretaries, and custodians are. Consequently, child care workers do not ordinarily receive health care benefits, nor are they eligible for the extensive pension programs operated by national church agencies.

Finally, national leadership has not attempted in any systematic way to coordinate and support child care services by providing information and referral. Such official noninvolvement in all aspects of church-housed child day care is something of a curiosity, considering the heavy involvement in day care of so many local parishes. Ordinarily, regional and national church jurisdictions take a keen interest in offering guidance and resources for local parishes on such matters. In this instance, however, the Church seems neither to have clearly perceived the extent of its involvement as a provider nor to have even considered its potential role in coordinating and supporting the development of services.

It is apparent that the Church could rather easily take a more active role in shaping the development of church-housed child day care if it wished to do so. Nearly all communions maintain elaborate structures within local, state, regional, and national jurisdictions. Such structures might easily be used to provide the rudiments of a child care delivery system. In the area of information and referral, for example, it would cost little to develop a communications system. Further consideration of the Church's potential as a delivery system and of issues that should be considered in evaluating possible new roles appears in the Epilogue.

This chapter and the next examine the current provision of church-housed child care in as much detail as possible in order to lay a foundation of knowledge to guide continuing discussions of potential new roles for the Church. Central to the design of the follow-up survey were concerns about the possible implications of the Church's taking *more* or *less* initiative to coordinate and support child care services: Are church-housed child care staff more isolated than other providers? Do they have less access to legislative information, program resources, or early childhood development materials than other providers? Are they paid less? Do they receive fewer benefits? Are their programs less accessible to the community? Do church-housed providers have less professional training? Are church-housed programs of lower quality as judged by prevailing standards? These and other questions concerning the strengths, weaknesses, and special needs of church-housed child day care guided the research program of the Child Day Care Project.

Why Is the Church Involved in Child Care?

While there is no simple answer to the question of why the Church has become so involved in child day care, local parishes have certain unique features that have made them particularly desirable locations for child care programs—available space, convenient community location, and tax-exempt status.

Space

Protestant and Orthodox churches belonging to the National Council of Churches have long been seriously committed to the development of buildings as an expression of their mission. Indeed, critics within the Church have sometimes lamented this "edifice complex." In turn, the Church has answered that it can better serve human needs by such works of brick and mortar. Whatever the ultimate reasons for real-estate acquisition and construction, it can safely be asserted that the Church is one of the most significant property owners in the country. Its buildings dot the skylines of virtually every town. Church architecture has expressed itself in a variety of ways from the spacious and dominant to the modest and circumspect, from Gothic cathedrals to urban settlement houses. During the post-World-War-II era, when America was preoccupied with education, economic prosperity, and the baby boom, many churches undertook programs of building expansion. Much of this activity was channeled into the erection of "educational wings" or classroom facilities built adjacent to the sanctuaries of parishes. When new church construction took place in the suburbs during the 1960s, original building plans called for the inclusion of classrooms, parish halls, all-purpose rooms, and fellowship halls. These buildings were added to the churches' already substantial property holdings in community buildings, settlement houses, and urban mission centers built in earlier years.

With their vast property holdings and historical patterns of construction, many parishes are well equipped to provide facilities for child care. Classrooms originally designed for Sunday school groups have child-sized fittings and furnishings—such as chairs, tables, toys, cribs, and changing tables—which are essential for child care programs. Moreover, this ideal space is generally available for child day care programs because most parishes use these facilities only for a few hours on Sunday or on other infrequent occasions when child care and education are offered to parents otherwise engaged in the life and worship of the church.

Because parishes have built buildings with a conscious attempt to serve the needs of families with children, they are particularly well suited to housing child care programs without expensive renovation. Thus the physical space intended to serve church members allows church members to serve the community.

One midwestern church with a congregation composed largely of elderly members makes its school rooms available, without cost, to a child care center. While none of the church members has preschool children, the pastor says that his church board views their building as a resource held in trust to be used for the community good.

A New Jersey pastor reported simply, "It is a part of our sense of being good neighbors. We want to offer our neighbors help in any way we can. Right now they need a place for their day care center."

Location

The convenience of church space for child care provision is further enhanced by church location within the community. The Church's universal presence creates a network of institutions that reaches deep into the life of all types of American communities. No matter how small the town, at least one church structure can be assured. In the colonial period of our history, the placement of the church was a serious consideration. A central town "green" was established with every important institution skirting its perimeter—the town hall, the bank, and the church. As the country grew in size and complexity, the church continued to occupy a strategic place in community planning and often was used as the demarcation between residential and commercial districts within a town. Having been early arrivals, churches became centrally located as communities grew up around them. Today many of them owe their prime locations to length of tenure within the community.

As suburban tracts and new cities were planned, it was not unusual for conveniently located corner plots to be left vacant to permit the development of community institutions, among them churches. The churches made excellent use of this space, which provided an accessible place for worship and for community services to area residents.

Both the presence of churches everywhere and their convenient location contributed to the development of child care programs within their buildings. Whatever a community's patterns and preferences for residence and employment, a church is close at hand: close to public transportation, along major city streets, nestled among housing projects. It is hard to imagine a person who does not pass a church while commuting to work.

An urban Florida parish made a self-conscious decision to remain in a downtown location during the late 1960s. Strongly influencing their decision to remain was a determination to provide services for city residents. Their location across from the central bus depot led them to develop day care for both preschoolers and the elderly. In this way family members could drop them at the church on their way to and from their employment.

Tax-exempt Status

In addition to their physical space and location, the churches offer an important financial advantage for provision of child care because of their exemption from taxes. In several ways, this factor facilitates the development of child care and other community service programs within churches. First, child care programs can simply be operated under the churches' non-profit articles of incorporation, eliminating the need to establish a new corporation. Second, costs are lower because no taxes are paid, yet churches receive city services: fire and police protection, garbage disposal, and so forth.

For individuals or groups seeking to start a child day care program or nursery school, tax-exempt status provides significant financial incentives to house the program in a church facility. One experienced child care provider says, "Even when other doors are closed in a community, churches will at least consider housing child care centers. The problems and start-up costs associated with opening are usually sharply reduced because the church already has equipment, insurance, and garbage collection. If the church is willing, the child care program can operate under the church's non-profit status."

Says another, "Anyone who stays in child care long enough will sooner or later work in a church—they're just the most convenient locations."

Thus space, location, and tax-exempt status all contribute to the desirability of church properties for child care programs. For some churches, these three factors are the *only* reasons for their having become involved in the provision of child day care. Even where churches provide subsidies to child care programs or where they operate their own programs, considerations of available space, prime location, and tax exemption have been decisive in the development of programs on church property.

Yet these factors alone do not explain the Church's major role as provider. Ultimately it is the willingness of the churches that makes the location of child care programs in church facilities possible. This willingness derives from the Church's views of its role in the community. Formally called *mission theology*, these conceptions provide the reasoning behind a church's decision to allow its buildings to be used for child care.

Ideas of Ministry

Like much in American religious life, there is no common agreement about involvement in local community service on the part of parishes. As a result, no simple universal portrait can be drawn of involvement in child care by local parishes. A variety of ideas of ministry shape the development of programs, and none of these notions of ministry excludes others. These ideas are generally not pure types, nor is the Church immune to a common human tendency to be less than clear about its motivation.

Among the conceptions or theologies of mission that inform the decision of a local parish to become involved in the provision of child care are those outlined on the following pages. Often these concepts work in conjunction with each other or provide only a partial basis for a parish's decision to be involved in child care.

Christian education. A nursery school or child day care program with an explicit religious education component may be part of the mission undertaken by a parish. When this is the motivation, spiritual development will be central to the program.

Pastoral care. Child care may be viewed as part of a larger program of care and nurture of families within the congregation. Again, religious teachings and/or values clarification may be part of the program. Congregations motivated to be involved with child care by concern for either Christian education or pastoral care will often, though not always, serve primarily children and families of their own membership.

Evangelism. Some programs of child care are viewed within a larger context of evangelism or proclamation of the Christian faith to those outside the congregation. Thus child care programs may be seen as a way of expanding the fellowship of the parish and ultimately increasing the membership.

Stewardship. All parishes make decisions regarding the allocation of their financial resources. Some view the physical plant and equipment as a trust that they must use in the larger expression of ministry as they best see it. Under this conception, child care may be viewed as an appropriate use whether by members or non-members.

Community service. Like stewardship conceptions, ideas of ministry related to community service hold that the church has some general responsibility to meet the needs of others. Under this conception, programs are likely to be open to persons outside of the membership. It is this view of ministry that often leads churches to respond positively to requests from child care directors to take up residence within the church building. A wide range of programs may be considered within this conception of ministry.

Social justice. Congregations that view themselves as having a significant role to play with regard to the promotion of social justice may introduce child care programs as part of that ministry. Often these programs serve particular populations, such as disabled children, single parents, low-income groups, or racial/ethnic minorities.

These six ideas of ministry by no means exhaust the possibilities that may influence congregations. Often these views overlap and are seen as complementary by church boards, pastors, and congregations. Perhaps even more frequently, different segments of the congregation will view the same child care program differently. For example, the pastor may see the program as good stewardship and as an opportunity for evangelism; the trustees may see it as a source of revenue; the Women's Guild may view it as a social justice program. At the same time, the parents may see the church merely as a landlord to the child care program. Occasionally, different views within a parish will actively compete with one another, possibly leading to serious confusion of purpose and even to unintentional negative effects on programs and participants. More often, such differences simply express themselves in a lack of clarity or intentionality with respect to child care programs housed in the church.

Whatever the guiding force, theology, or rationale, local churches have increasingly reached out to families in their parishes and communities to carry on a significant ministry of child care. This ministry can be as varied as the philosophies, income levels, racial and ethnic backgrounds, and special needs of the families served and, indeed, as varied as the concepts of ministry that motivate a congregation to open its doors to a child care program in the first place. To understand and view the Church as provider, then, means to evaluate both the unique features it possesses as a social institution as well as to appreciate something of its theological processes, since it is these that lend hue and form to the stained glass windows on child care.

How Have Local Parishes Become Involved in Child Care?

The characteristics of location, space, and tax-exempt status together with theologies of mission help to explain the general *desirability* of churches as sites for child care programs and the general *receptivity* of churches to housing or directly providing such programs. But to understand how particular programs came to exist in particular parishes, one must take a closer, more personalized look. Though each child care program has its own unique history, the Child Day Care Project sought to identify common strands that have produced the complex weave now so characteristic of church-housed child care.

Early in the study it became apparent that church-housed child care is best understood in each case as a grassroots phenomenon. As pointed out earlier, the Church, as an institution, did not consciously decide to become a provider of child care. Rather, local churches responded to local needs within their congregations and communities as well as to their own ethic, thereby creating a broad pattern of services housed in churches in every state and community of this country.

Local churches often participate actively in developing solutions to problems facing their communities. Sometimes the problem-solving is initiated by such groups as the League of Women Voters, human service planning committees, family service agencies, and community action groups. They form committees that identify local needs, then seek funds and accessible locations for programs to meet these needs. Committees, which usually include pastors and church members, quickly recognize the appropriateness of church facilities for play groups, nursery schools, mothers' support programs, parent education seminars, or day care centers.

In a less formalized fashion, a church member or local citizen may initiate with the pastor or church group a proposal that church space be used to operate a child care program. Similarly, community groups may apply for "deacons' funds" or other sources of funding available through local congregations to meet the child care needs they have identified. Often child care programs seek funds from congregations to use for program start-up, new equipment, scholarships to low-income families, better wages for staff, or new program components. In addition to or instead of financial resources, a church may provide in-kind support to child care. Through women's groups or other church organizations, volunteers are sought to serve on boards, to write proposals and press releases, to donate and repair equipment, and to provide accounting services and assistance in the classroom.

In a Kansas community, two child care programs were initiated many years ago with broad community support from the League of Women Voters, several churches, and a number of civic organizations. In this instance, church and community joined hands in a cooperative response to the needs of their young working mothers. The programs' budgets today reflect continuing support from those founding organizations. In turn, the two centers serve five youngsters with handicaps and provide a worksite for senior citizen volunteers who tell stories, play games, and rock children on their laps. Also, the center's director has been a significant part of an effort to develop child-abuse prevention programs for six midwestern states.

Sometimes availability of child care in a given church is the result of pressure exerted by parishioners who have family needs. Young parents—eagerly seeking parenting skills, emotional support, or socialization experiences for their youngsters—organize cooperative playgroups or programs for "mother's morning out." Parent participation is not always as apparent as it once was. Divorce, separation, and economic pressures have created growing numbers of single, working parents and two-earner families for whom appropriate and affordable child day care services are a necessity rather than a luxury. For such reasons, many church-operated and church-initiated programs have experienced unusually rapid evolution from mothers' support groups to comprehensive, full-day programs for children.

Major Types of Child Care Programs Offered

Responses to the initial questionnaire revealed a broad range of program offerings in church locations. The findings reported in Table 2 indicate that programs for children of preschool age are far and away the most prevalent. It is important to note in this context that multiple program offerings within a single church are usually operated as one. Thus, the "programs" referred to in Table 2 and elsewhere represent the different types of services offered within a church—for example, care for toddlers, preschoolers, and school-age children before or after school—rather than administratively distinct child care operations. In the remainder of this book, "center" refers to all programs operating under the same management structure.

Programs reported as "other" in the initial questionnaire of the Child Day Care Project often are pioneering programs seeking to serve some of society's neediest and most difficult-to-place children. These programs, especially, set in relief the pressing needs of America's families for assistance in caring for young children. Examples of such programs are described on page 26 under the heading "Samaritan Child Care." However, even the more readily classifiable programs noted in Table 2 represent a wide variety of responses to community and parish needs. Some illustrations follow.

A large black congregation in a southwestern city, seeking to serve the needs of its own parishioners who required daytime care for their toddlers, developed a program stressing religious teachings and affirmation of black culture. The church soon discovered a need to add infant

Table 2

Distribution of Programs by Type Based on
Responses to the Initial Survey
(8,767 Respondents; 14,589 Programs)

Program Type	Number of Programs Reported	Type as % of All Programs
Infant Programs	903	6%
Toddler Programs	1,935	13%
Preschool Programs	7,272	50%
Disabled Children	326	2%
Before/After School	1,276	9%
Emergency Drop-off	421	3%
Mother's Support Program	1,528	11%
Other	928	6%
Total Programs	14,589	100%

care and preschool components to the program. Within the initial year of operation, the center expanded to provide care from 6:00 a.m. to 7:00 p.m., five days a week, for children from two months to six years of age, including a kindergarten program. As the program grew in size and scope, the sponsoring congregation became more aware of and committed to the child care needs of the larger community. During the first 18 months of operation, the congregation contributed the space, many volunteers, and $50,000 that was used for supplies, equipment, and building alterations.

Other churches respond less to a specific need among parishioners than to injustices in society at large. They advocate for their church to develop or support programs for abused children, for disabled children, or for children caught in the destructive web of conditions that poverty spins.

A program for abused children in an Ozark mountain community of Arkansas found itself bereft of a location. In desperation, the director spoke to his pastor about the program's needs. Together they approached the church vestry, and soon the program was housed within the church. It was not an easy transition for the parish, because troubled children are often hard on equipment and the building, and their behavior may be disruptive. The pastor, committed to the program, preached to and counseled his congregation. Slowly their objections diminished, and ownership, even pride, in the program began to flourish.

In a small city on the fringe of Boston, a large Head Start program also floundered for lack of permanent and appropriate space. Two churches and a synagogue moved into this void, offering spacious, attractive, and well-equipped facilities to house the program.

As the programs grow and evolve in response to grassroots pressures and needs, their purposes and structures reflect local lifestyles and work behaviors. A Montana resort community experiences high unemployment except during the tourist season. During that brief period when work is available to parents, child day care is essential. Local churches have worked together to provide full-day child care programs during those months. One parish offers infant care, another toddler care, and so on, to meet the community's child care needs. Although this coordinated program operates only four months a year, it provides a vital service to the community and a ministry in support of families.

A child care center that opens its doors at 6:00 a.m. or 6:30 a.m. will often be located in a neighborhood or small town where parents work in a hospital or factory on an early morning shift. In a northeastern industrial city, working parents of young children had to report for a 7:00 a.m. shift. They needed before-school care so that children could be assured of breakfast and supervision from the time parents left for work until their children left for school an hour and a half later. Working with community groups and the school district, two parishes sponsored a before-school program and arranged for school buses to pick up the children at their doors. Local health officials reported a decline in pediatric hospital admissions following the initiation of these programs. Doubtless, parents now work with greater peace of mind knowing that their children are not alone at home trying to make breakfast.

In rural areas where families are isolated geographically, cooperative playgroups help reduce isolation for child and parent alike. In a rural, upstate New York village, a small church opened its doors to provide a playgroup for several children in the area. The playgroup experience offered important socialization opportunities for these young children isolated by accident of geography. The playgroup also benefited parents—some trapped at home with no transportation, distant neighbors, and little money; others depressed by temporary unemployment that was depleting both their financial and their emotional resources. Coming together in the playgroup allowed these mothers to share parenting and homemaking skills and concerns, and perhaps most important, to lend much-needed emotional support to one another, thereby stabilizing, even strengthening, family life for children.

As a church works to identify the needs of children and families and involves itself more in meeting those needs, it begins to concern itself with the broader health and welfare of the community. This may lead the church to strengthen and make more accessible other community and church services, such as food banks, counseling programs, job training, and housing services. Though the impetus for child care programs may come from outside the parish, many churches have become providers through their willing response to expressions of community need.

Although the Child Day Care Project studied programs, not children or families, the findings of the study—drawn from interviews and visits as well as questionnaires—provide us with more than a glimpse into the lives of those served. One particular concern when undertaking this study was that churches would be found to serve mainly the children of their own congregations. As the preceding thumbnail sketches suggest, this concern was unfounded. In fact, responses to the initial questionnaire indicated that 99% of all programs were open to all members of the community. Not surprisingly, the program type that is most likely to be restricted to members of the congregation is "mothers' support program." Still, 94% of these do not require church membership. In short, the vast majority of church-housed child day care programs can be viewed as programs for the community, whether operated by a church or only based in church property.

Samaritan Child Care: Refusing to Pass on the Other Side

The programs classified as "other" in responses to the initial questionnaire represent a remarkable array of child care services. We learned about the nature of these programs through unsolicited information that accompanied responses to both the initial and follow-up questionnaires. The follow-up survey was particularly revealing. Over 100 program directors indicated in letters that they could not complete the standard questionnaire for their programs, then went on to describe, often painstakingly and poignantly, the specialized forms of child care they provide.

Invariably directors would tell us that their programs had simply sprung up because of an urgent need of a small minority of families in their communities. In most cases it was convincingly explained that for these families there is nowhere else to turn. For the churches that respond to these needs, it is less a matter of systematically deciding to undertake a program in child care—although some of these programs are surprisingly complex and sophisticated—than it is a situation reminiscent of the Biblical parable of the Good Samaritan—that is, a perceived need and a decision to act. In the next few pages, we share some of their stories, for they are illustrative of the wide expanse of child care needs. For those of us caught up in the great struggle to provide programs of quality care to the "normal" population of young children, it is important to remember from time to time the greater struggles of society's more marginal children and families—of whom Hubert Humphrey once said, "They live in the shadows of life."

A rural congregation in southern New Jersey provides care 14 hours per day, six days per week for the three months that the berry and corn crops are harvested. The children of migrant workers come to the church, where volunteers provide supervision, meals, and the rudiments of a program from 5:30 a.m. – 7:00 p.m.: "Each day, 'enrollment' is different in members and age range. We accept donations from parents for the service and offer them free clothes (for the children) which we collect all year. We tell them too about free health care and other social services that they can use while they are in the area. I guess you could say our goal is to provide a safe environment for children so that their parents can be free for work or other activities."

An Oklahoma City parish uses a volunteer staff to operate a program of respite care for five hours per day, Monday through Thursday, eight months per year. This program is for mentally retarded and emotionally disturbed children and is intended as a ministry to their families in allowing them a short break from the 24-hour-per-day care they must provide for their children. Charging $1.50 per hour (to pay for supplies), the program does not have a formal enrollment process and is more of a drop-off program: "Our program allows parents to get other errands done. Most come twice a week for about two to three hours.... If they are here during lunch their mothers send the food—many have special dietary needs. We usually have four to six children at any one time. Most are under six but some are as old as 30. We sing, play games, read stories, and go to our playground. The mothers really like to meet each other and talk, over a cup of coffee.... It isn't really child care but we think it is an important program."

Many programs operated on an intergenerational basis wrote to us. Sometimes these programs just evolve in a church where both child care and day care for elderly persons are offered. A portion of the day's program is operated with young and old together, with positive outcomes for both. In Carlsbad, New Mexico, one church offers a program for three hours, twice per month. This program is without cost and mothers take turns providing a snack: "...we give them some grandmother relationships. Many of the young families in our church are far from their original homes and they feel the lack of grandparents in their extended families."

An intergenerational program in Florida stresses the importance to elderly men who join the program as volunteers, working one morning per week: "Great friendships are formed and there are sad faces when summer arrives and a three-month holiday begins."

Other communities respond to local or regional realities that create special needs for child care. For example, a Texas Gulf-Coast town provides a drop-in center/mothers' support group for the families of workers gone long months to work on oil rigs.

In Wyoming, the influx of families due to an upswing in uranium mining has brought with it new needs for child care: "Our program was begun a few years ago in response to the large number of grade school children in our community who have working mothers. Our town is a highly affluent city of just over 50,000, with a very high proportion of young families who work in energy-related fields. Many families have been highly mobile and there is an extremely high divorce rate. We would like to get more involved in serving the needs of parents."

Another Florida congregation has trained elderly volunteers to provide respite care for children who are chronically or terminally ill as a support service to parents: "...without such support the parents just naturally begin to withdraw emotionally from children they will soon lose. Our volunteers are moving toward the end of life, too. They can relate to these children.... Of course, we don't have any regular time schedule or enrollment. There is no charge."

Finally, there is the rural church in the foothills of the Rocky Mountains: "Two years ago the ladies of our church decided to have a sort of Child Care Center at our church for the children of the people who pick the local cherry crop—which lasts from a few days to 10 or 12 days. The pickers get into the cherry orchard as early as 4:00 a.m. Their small children have to stay in the cars or under the trees while their parents, grandparents, and older brothers or sisters pick cherries. Sometimes it is terribly hot. We go to the orchard between 7:30 a.m. and 8:00 a.m., pick up the children who will go with us, and take them to our educational building. There we serve them cookies and punch. At 11:30 a.m. we serve them an appropriate lunch consisting of sandwiches, a hot dish, relishes, cheese, fruit, and punch or milk. Their parents pick them up before 2:00 p.m. or 3:00 p.m.... Our church members, both old and young, take care of the children and furnish the food and other necessities. We sometimes have very small babies to care for. We set a limit to ages five or six."

Many other illustrations could be given, but these programs give an indication of instances in which churches, like the Good Samaritan, encounter another traveler much afflicted by life's trials, and like the Samaritan, they choose not to pass by on the other side. These Samaritans need and deserve the attention and support of the Church as well as of the day care community.

As national church agencies move toward the formulation of more detailed and intentional policies and programs of child care, it must be with a heightened consciousness of the full breadth of program types and styles. As "Samaritan child care" programs well illustrate, child care needs within communities are diverse and changeable, necessitating a high degree of flexibility within social institutions, such as the Church, that seek to meet these needs.

III
The Nature of Church-Housed Child Day Care: Follow-up Survey Findings

This chapter presents information gathered during a second, follow-up survey of selected parishes of the 15 denominations participating in the study. The lengthy questionnaire developed for this phase of the Child Day Care Project is reproduced in Appendix 2. Though at first glance it might seem to raise all of the questions anyone would ever want to ask about church-housed child day care, in fact, it is more on the order of the preliminary questions you might ask to engage a new acquaintance in conversation. As with any first meeting, we come away from the follow-up survey feeling closer to the subject than before, but very much aware of how much remains to be learned.

The first section of this chapter—Research Design and Method—contains a nontechnical description and discussion of the research design and methodology of this phase of the study. The next nine sections (beginning on page 37) present detailed findings from the follow-up survey, organized by a series of questions the study sought to answer, such as "Who is served by church-housed programs?" and "How do churches contribute to the programs they house?" The final section—Major Findings (beginning on page 73)—summarizes the extensive information from preceding sections into sketches comparing different types of centers and programs housed in church buildings: *church-operated centers* versus *independently operated centers*; *for-profit centers* versus *non-profit centers*; and *part-time preschool programs* versus *full-time preschool programs*.

Research Design and Method

Before reporting the findings of the study, we describe the general methods of the follow-up survey, to explain the ways in which information from the questionnaire is analyzed and presented and to state the research questions that organize the presentation. Footnotes present more detailed discussions of particular issues that may be of interest to some readers.

Survey Methods

The sample of child day care program directors to receive the second questionnaire was selected from the pool of directors named by respondents to the first questionnaire.[4] The follow-up survey sample was substantially smaller than the total number of respondents to the initial survey because resources of the Child Day Care Project dictated a maximum sample size of 3,500.[5] Ultimately, a total of 3,361 questionnaires were mailed in the follow-up survey.[6] Of these, 3,333 were delivered, and 1,506 were returned in usable form by the cut-off date of September 10, 1982. The overall rate of response to the follow-up survey was 45%.

The sampling design that we employed for the follow-up survey (see footnote, preceding) was intended to substantially under-represent the program type most commonly reported in the first survey (preschool programs) and to over-represent less common types (e.g., infant programs). Alas, our rather complicated intentions were not realized. In fact, any sampling procedure that relied (as ours did) on pastors' classifica-

---

[4]The Project schedule made it necessary to select the sample for the follow-up survey before all responses to the first survey had been received. The sample was drawn in May 1982, when roughly two thirds of the total responses to the first questionnaire had been received and processed.

[5]The sampling procedure was fairly complicated. First, we decided to include *all* centers (234 as of the sampling) identified in the initial survey that were associated with the seven smallest denominations (see Table 1, page 13). This was done to ensure some representation from these denominations in the final sample—a goal just barely achieved, since five of the seven small denominations each sent fewer than five responses to the follow-up questionnaire. Second, we decided to include all infant programs (819 as of the sampling) and all disabled children's programs (294 as of the sampling), given their low incidence (6% and 2% of all programs, respectively), their increasing policy relevance, and the relative lack of information about such programs in the literature. Third, we selected an additional 2,153 centers from the remaining pool of responses to the initial survey, to bring the total sample size to 3,500. This selection was accomplished by stratified random sampling procedures designed (1) to ensure a minimum representation of 50 centers from each of the eight larger denominations, (2) to give selection priority to centers for which directors had been identified by name, and (3) to produce the following proportional representation of program types in the total sample: toddler programs, 25%; preschool programs, 20%; before/after school programs, 6%; emergency drop-off, mothers' support, and "other" programs, each 4%.

[6]The drop from 3,500 centers originally selected was caused by eliminating duplicate names/addresses from the mailing list. Duplication occurred in the first place because some persons had been identified as directors of more than one program associated with a single church-housed center.

tions of programs operating in their churches would have been similarly frustrated, for what pastors claimed to be the programs housed in their churches and what the follow-up survey revealed to be the actual programs housed in their churches, according to child day care center directors, were often quite different.

So, what can be said of the relationship between our sample and the total population of child day care programs in the churches of participating denominations? First, particular program types may be somewhat over- or under- represented in our sample; we simply do not know. Second, in light of the random sampling within program types and the high (45%) rate of response to the follow-up survey, it seems very likely that the programs described are representative of those currently being operated among all churches of the participating denominations.

Our discovery that pastors are not particularly reliable sources of information about the child day care programs operating in their parishes lends strong support to arguments made in the preceding chapter that child day care in churches is not the result of organized development by Church leadership at any level. Certainly if it were the outcome of a formal program of the Church—as is true of Sunday school programs, for example—pastors would be more knowledgeable than they are. Only by directly approaching day care providers in the follow-up survey were we able to paint a detailed picture of church-housed child care.

Data Analysis and Presentation of Findings

The relation between questions asked in the questionnaire and the questions or variables analyzed here is not always straightforward. For example, the questionnaire asks, "At what hour does your preschool program open?", "At what hour does it close?", and "How many days per week does this program operate?" However, before analyzing data from the follow-up questionnaire, we combined responses to these three questions into a single variable— "number of hours per week that program operates." For this reason we have labeled the first column in the tables that follow "Question/Variable," reflecting the fact that instead of analyzing responses to a single question, we sometimes analyze variables constructed from the responses to several questions.

It is important to note that the responses to some questions were not analyzed and are not reported in this volume. When the pattern or the proportion of responses to a question suggested that many respondents were unable to answer it or that different respondents made very different sense of it, we gave responses to the question no further consideration in the study.[7] In addition, after several unsatisfactory attempts to classify and quantify open-ended responses to several questions (57–59 in Appendix 2), we decided instead to present a sampling of them in the form of verbatim quotations. These quotes appear in Chapter IV — The Voices of Providers.

The presentation of findings from the follow-up survey is organized around a series of research questions about the nature of church-housed child day care. These are listed in the final section of this chapter introduction. As each question is considered, we first answer it for *all* church-housed centers. Generally, the percentage of centers giving each answer is presented. Occasionally, responses are also summarized by presenting the mean, or average, response to a particular question—for example, the average weekly fee paid by parents for child care, expressed in dollars. The total number of responses to particular questions seldom equals the total number of respondents (1,506), since typically some persons failed to respond or did not provide usable responses. Finally, it should be noted that the percents for different categories of response to particular questions do not always sum to 100% due to rounding errors.

Three contrasts. Besides answering each research question for church-housed centers as a group, we also compare different types of providers *within* the total sample. Three contrasts are investigated: First, we divide the total sample into centers classified as *church-operated* and centers classified as *independently operated*, and contrast the responses from these two groups. Next, we redivide the total sample into *for-profit* centers and *non-profit* centers and contrast responses from these two groups. Finally, we contrast responses from *part-time preschool* programs and *full-time preschool* programs (preschool programs being only a sub-sample of the total sample of church-housed programs).

Figure 1 illustrates these divisions into contrasting types of centers/programs. It is apparent from Figure 1 that in each division, the feature used to contrast centers/programs does not produce two groups of equal size. There are, for example, many more non-profit centers (90% of the total sample) than for-profit centers (10% of the total sample) among all church-housed centers surveyed. Operational definitions and brief discussions of each contrast follow.

---

[7] In spite of having pretested the follow-up questionnaire with a small sample of child day care center directors and having revised questions in light of this experience, we found that some questions in the final version of the questionnaire did not elicit usable information. Occasionally the structured response categories of the questionnaire did not adequately reflect the complexity of the real world of church-housed child day care. Not finding a response option that described their situation, some respondents refused to answer; some wrote marginal notes (or essays) that educated Project staff but could not be coded; and still others answered as best they could, given the options provided, but in so doing misconstrued their actual situations. Some questions were simply confusing or required information that many or most directors did not have.

Figure 1

Division of Church-Housed Child Day Care Centers into Contrasting Types

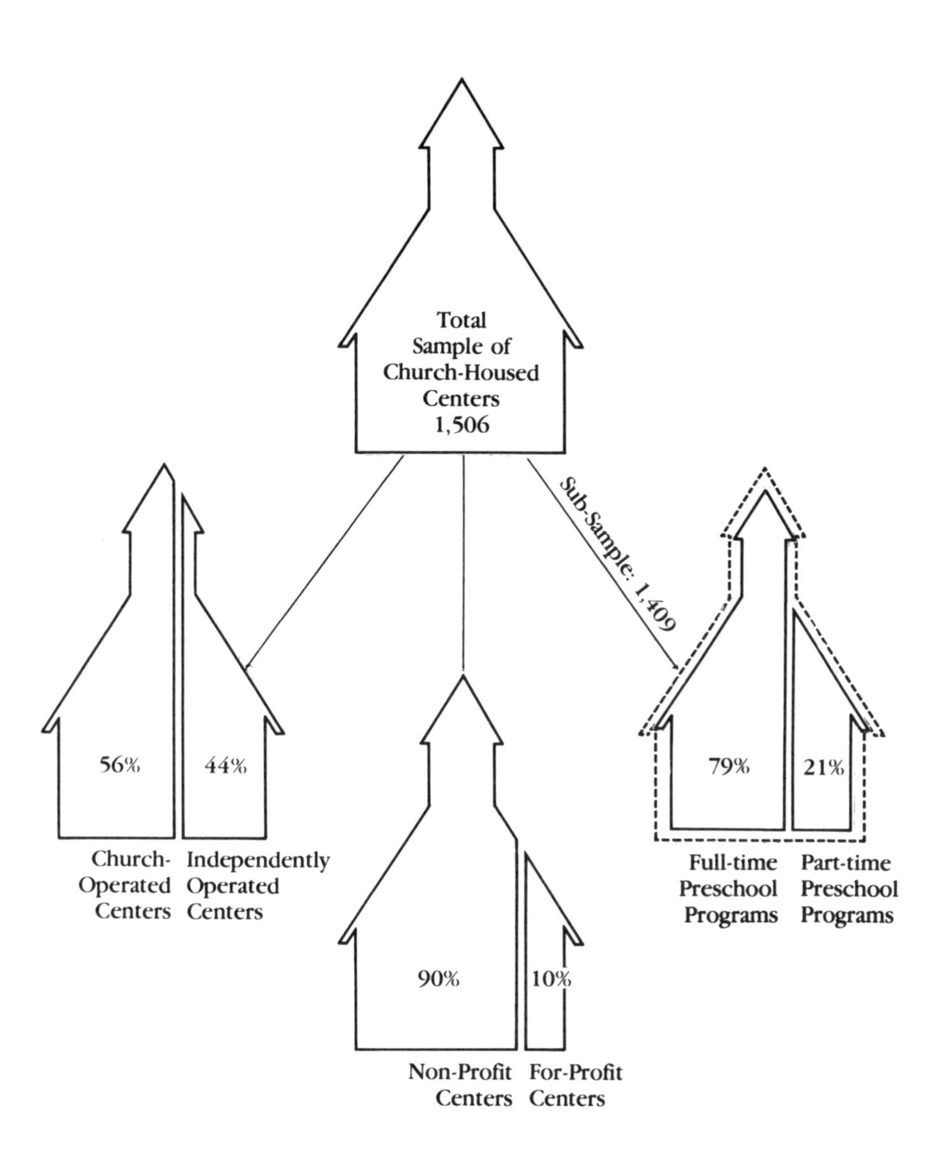

Church-operated versus independently operated centers. Among child care centers housed in the churches surveyed, some are formally administered by the church/congregation, and others occupy church property under rental or use agreements but are administratively autonomous. In some instances, the administrative relationship between church and center is clear: a center operated under the incorporation of the church and directly managed by the church board is *church-operated*; a Head Start center operated by a public corporation that pays rent to the church for the use of indoor and outdoor space is *independently operated*. In many instances, however, the relationship between church and center is somewhat ambiguous. For example, a center may have been founded by a member of the congregation and operated informally (and perhaps unconsciously) under the umbrella of church incorporation for several years but never have been directly administered by the church board. Indeed, it may even have formed an independent "board of directors" including persons who have nothing to do with the church. Should such a program be considered church-operated or independently operated? An enormous variety of relationships exist between child day care centers and the churches in which they are located.

Ultimately the decision as to whether a center would be considered church-operated or independently operated was left to the judgment of pastors: the classification was made according to their responses to the initial questionnaire. Thus, what in reality is a continuum of relationship was broken into two parts: one representing *closer* relation to the church; the other, *more distant* relation. Fifty-six percent of centers were classified as church-operated; 44%, as independently operated.

For-profit versus non-profit centers. Regarding the classification of centers into *for-profit* and *non-profit* groups, it is important to note that the distinction was *not* made on the basis of type of incorporation. Rather, centers were classified according to directors' responses to a question (32b, Appendix 2) that asked, "Is your child day care program a proprietorship (owner-operated, for-profit)?" Only 8% of directors responded "yes"; 74% responded "no"; and 18% did not respond at all. Those responding "yes" were classified as for-profit centers, while those responding "no" were classified as non-profit centers. Thus, the for-profit/non-profit contrast reflects directors' perceptions of whether their centers are business enterprises.[8]

---

[8] In fact, some operations treated as business enterprises by the IRS probably appear in the ranks of so-called non-profits. For example, small centers operated by individuals with little or no capital investment and no papers of incorporation might well be misclassified. One can imagine such a respondent thinking, "I'm not doing this to make money. I guess I should answer 'no'."

Of the three contrasts investigated, this one produced the most unbalanced groups with respect to size. Ninety percent (1,121) of centers responding were classified as *non-profit*; only 10% (119), as *for-profit*.[9]

Part-time versus full-time preschool programs. Programs for children of preschool age (three- and four-year-olds) are offered by 95% of the centers surveyed, while only 45% offer toddler programs (for 18- to 36-month-olds) and 29% offer infant programs (for 0- to 24-month-olds). A common perception at the beginning of the study was that many church-housed centers would serve only preschoolers in programs following traditional part-day nursery school formats. In fact, church-housed centers responding to the survey enroll rather large numbers of infants, toddlers, and even school-age children in before- and after-school programs. However, there is no doubt that they serve more preschoolers than children in other age groups, which is also the case with center-based programs nationally.[10] As for the hypothesis that church-housed preschool programs would generally follow traditional part-day nursery school formats, preliminary analyses revealed that a majority of preschool programs operate on extended schedules that might be considered full-day.

In this chapter, programs operating for 30 or more hours per week are designated *full-time*; programs operating for fewer than 30 hours per week, *part-time*.[11] Very few programs fall at or near the 30 hour per week cut point— most either operate for 15 or fewer hours per week or for 45 or more hours per week. It should be noted that even programs offering full-day care five days per week may serve children who are enrolled for only part of the day and/or week, spending the rest of their time in the care of their parents and/or other caregivers. Likewise, programs offering part-time care may serve children who are actually receiving full-time care outside their homes in a combination of settings.

---

[9]The number of for-profit centers is so small that care should be taken in generalizing from what may be an extremely unusual sample of for-profit operations to the much larger population of for-profits housed outside the church.

[10]Coelen, C., Glantz, F., & Calore, D. *Day care centers in the U.S.: A national profile 1976-1977*. Cambridge, MA: Abt Books, 1979. Chorvinsky, M. *Preprimary enrollment 1980*. Washington, DC: National Center for Education Statistics, 1982.

[11]Rather than distinguishing "part-day" from "full-day" programs, we decided to contrast programs according to the maximum number of hours of care provided for individual children during an operating week. The selection of a cut point was guided by current thinking in the field of child day care, which suggests that programs operating for 30 or more hours per week are more likely to be used for full-time care, or as a significant component of full-time care, by working parents.

When the sub-sample comprised of centers offering preschool programs (95% of the total sample) was divided according to the 30 hour per week criterion, programs classified as *part-time* constituted 21% of the sub-sample; *full-time* programs, 79%. As with the preceding two contrasts, numerous differences were found between centers/programs in the two groups, differences that suggest the intended contrast was achieved in spite of imperfect and surely debatable, classification.[12]

One last note regarding data analysis is necessary. When different types of centers are contrasted, their responses are described as "different" *only* when statistical tests indicate that they are reliably different. More specifically, only when it is 95% or more certain that absolute differences between groups did not occur by *chance* do we describe the groups as "different."[13]

Research Questions

The remainder of this chapter presents and discusses findings from the second, follow-up survey. The presentation is organized by a series of questions about the nature of church-housed child day care:

- Who is served?
- What services are provided?
- What are the goals of church-housed programs?
- Who provides child care services?
- What can be said about program quality?
- How are programs administered?
- What are the sources of income and the expenses of centers?
- How do churches contribute to centers?
- How do church-housed providers relate to church and community?

In addressing each question, we first present and discuss information for the total sample of church-housed centers and programs. Next, we present findings for the three pairs of contrasted sub-samples—church-operated versus independently operated centers; for-profit versus non-profit centers; and part-time versus full-time preschool programs. Tables sum-

---

[12]Besides comparing preschool programs operating for 30 hours or more per week with ones operating less than 30 hours per week, we also compared (1) programs operating 45 or more hours per week with ones operating less than 45 hours per week and (2) programs operating 45 or more hours per week with ones operating less than 16 hours per week. The findings were virtually identical in all three cases, due to the concentration of cases at the tails of the distribution.

[13]Actual probabilities, or significance levels, are indicated where the findings for each contrast are presented in Appendices 3 through 5. Chi square was used to test for differences between response distributions; Student's *t* statistic, for differences between means.

marizing the responses from the total sample appear in this chapter. Tables summarizing the responses for the three pairs of contrasted sub-samples appear in Appendices 3 through 5.

Suffer the Little Children to Come: Who Is Served?

Although both phases of the study were concerned primarily with obtaining information about programs rather than about children and their families, the follow-up questionnaire sheds some light on who is served by church- housed child day care programs. Available information is summarized in Table 3 for the total study sample; detailed results for sub-sample contrasts are presented in Appendices 3 through 5.

As was discovered in the initial survey, very few church-housed centers (less that 2%) restrict enrollment to children of church members. One third of the responding centers serve at least some families who receive public assistance as indexed by the center's receipt of state or federal subsidies for serving such families. And as information in a later section indicates, a majority of centers make an effort to serve lower-income families by making scholarships and/or sliding-scale fees available.

The ethnic composition of children enrolled in church- housed programs is difficult for us to evaluate in relation to children in the national population or to children in child day care programs nationally, given published statistics. The obstacles to comparison are basically classificatory, arising from different definitions of ethnic/racial groups (as in the classification of Hispanics), inclusion/exclusion of particular child care settings (center/home), consideration of different program types ("educational" versus "custodial"), and so on. The percent of minority children enrolled in church-housed programs appears to be quite similar to the percent among three- and four-year-olds enrolled in "private preprimary" education programs nationally in 1980, but less than the percent of minority children enrolled in preprimary programs classified as "public"[14] and less than the percent of minority children of all ages enrolled in *licensed* center-based day care nationally in 1976–77.[15] It would not be particularly surprising to find that the percent of minority children at-

---

[14] Chorvinsky, op. cit., p. 4.

[15] U.S. Bureau of the Census. Money income and poverty status of families and persons in the United States: 1981. *Current Population Reports*. Series P-60, No. 134, July 1982.

Table 3
Who Is Served?
Findings from the Follow-up Survey for the
Total Sample of Church-Housed Child Day Care Centers
(Total Sample Size = 1,506)

Question/Variable	Responses	Total *Number* of Centers Responding
1. Is church membership required for program admittance?		*1,506*
yes	1.5%	
no	98.5%	
2. Are any families receiving public assistance?		*1,506*
yes	32.7%	
no	67.3%	
3. Ethnic composition of children enrolled (mean %):		*1,168*
White (not Hispanic)	85.2%	
Black (not Hispanic)	8.1%	
Hispanic	3.9%	
Asian	2.6%	
Native American	0.3%	
4. Type of community served:		*1,428*
central core of major city	12.1%	
fringe of major city	15.8%	
suburb of major city	24.7%	
small city (10,000-50,000)	25.1%	
small town or village	17.2%	
rural farming community	3.9%	
rural non-farm community	1.2%	
5. Number of children enrolled:		
a. Infant programs		*412*
total enrollment	6,072	
[mean enrollment]	[14.7]	
b. Toddler programs		*630*
total enrollment	11,586	
[mean enrollment]	[18.4]	
c. Preschool programs		*1,374*
total enrollment	61,620	
[mean enrollment]	[44.8]	
d. Centers		*1,455*
total enrollment	79,278	
[mean enrollment]	[54.5]	

tending church-housed programs in the study sample was actually somewhat lower than in a representative national sample. Such a finding would likely reflect the fact that nearly all denominations participating in this study are grossly under-represented in major inner-city areas where minority populations, particularly black Americans, are disproportionately concentrated.[16] In addition, churches infrequently house large, publicly funded programs like Head Start, which are most likely to enroll minority children.

It was not possible to compute the total number of children served by all types of programs housed in the churches responding to the survey; however, total enrollment figures are available for infant (6,072), toddler (11,586), and preschool (61,620) programs. Given the exploratory nature of this study, we feel justified in cautiously speculating about the number of children served by all church-housed programs among participating denominations. Of course, any attempt to generalize from the findings of the follow-up survey to the universe of parishes originally contacted—87,562 in all—must be tentative.

Nevertheless, by making several assumptions, it is possible to estimate a range within which the total number of infants, toddlers, and preschoolers served by all 87,562 parishes almost certainly falls. First, we assume that the average (mean) number of children enrolled per program (infant, toddler, or preschool) among *respondents* to the follow-up survey represents the average number of children enrolled by *all* churches that offer such programs—14.7 infants, 18.4 toddlers, and 44.8 preschoolers per program. Second, we assume that out of the total universe of 87,562 churches contacted in the initial survey, the number that actually reported offering each program type is the smallest possible number of churches offering each type: 903 infant programs, 1,935 toddler programs, and 7,272 preschool programs (Table 2, page 24). Third, we assume that, in the participating denominations, the maximum number of churches offering each program type is proportional to the number of churches offering each type among those responding to the initial questionnaire. This would mean that for the universe of 87,562 churches originally contacted, the estimated maximum numbers of infant, toddler, and preschool programs are 3,154 (or 3.6% of 87,562), 6,759 (7.7%), and 25,400 (29%), respectively.

Given these three assumptions, it is safe to conclude that the combined churches of the 15 denominations participating in this study enroll

---

[16] Ruopp, R., Travers, J., Glantz, F., & Coelen, C. *Children at the center: Summary findings and their implications* (Final report of the National Day Care Study, Volume 1). Cambridge, MA: Abt Associates, Inc., 1979.

bined churches of the 15 denominations participating in this study enroll between 375,000 and 1,309,000 infants, toddlers, and preschoolers in day care programs nationwide: 13,274–46,364 infants; 35,604–124,366 toddlers; and 325,786–1,137,920 preschoolers. By any standard both our minimum and maximum estimates are very large. The estimated numbers of preschoolers enrolled is particularly striking. Indeed, the 15 denominations represented in this study appear to provide day care for between 5% and 20% of three- and four-year-olds in the United States (roughly six million total). Moreover, since not all preschool-age children receive regular out-of-home care, the percentage of preschool-age children receiving day care who are enrolled in church-housed programs must be substantially greater. Certainly, inclusion of children participating in before/after school programs and receiving occasional care in conjunction with mothers' support programs or emergency drop-off programs would further inflate our estimates of the total number of children served. Finally, it should be remembered that our estimates pertain only to the 15 denominations surveyed. One can only guess at how many children are cared for by programs operating in all of America's churches—surely millions.

Church-Operated Versus Independently Operated Centers

Although church-operated and independently operated centers are equally *unlikely* to require church membership for admission to their programs, in other respects they do differ. Independently operated programs are more likely to serve families who receive public assistance and are somewhat more likely to enroll black children. Both of these differences most probably reflect not the existence of exclusionary rules but the evolution of many church-operated programs in response to the particular child care needs of their congregations. As indicated in the previous chapters, the denominations participating in the study comprise predominantly white, middle-class congregations, and many parishes first become involved in child day care to meet the immediate needs of church members rather than to serve the larger community. Findings from the follow-up survey also revealed that church-operated centers more often than independently operated centers are found in larger, more densely populated communities—communities having larger churches, more able and likely to initiate their own programs at the behest of church members. Regarding enrollment levels, church-operated toddler and preschool programs enroll more children than independently operated programs, and total enrollments are also higher among church-operated centers (61 versus 48 children per center).

For-Profit Versus Non-Profit Centers

Compared with for-profit centers, non-profit centers are more likely to serve families who receive public assistance, who belong to minority groups, and who live in larger, more densely populated communities. The first two differences would seem predictable on purely economic grounds. The third may also be a product of market forces—smaller communities offering market niches less conducive to the development of large, competitive, non-profit operations. These center types also differ with respect to enrollment levels—non-profit centers enrolling more infants and preschoolers, as well as more children of all ages (56 versus 41 children per center) than for-profit centers.

Part-time Versus Full-time Preschool Programs

Part-time preschool programs are more likely (4%) than full-time programs (1%) to restrict enrollment to members of the church in which they are located. In spite of this statistically significant difference, the total number of "restrictive" programs involved is extremely small—22 of the 1,409 responding; 13 of 294 part-time programs; 9 of 1,115 full-time programs. (It is worth remembering here the admonitions of some experts who, at the outset of the study, suggested that the survey was likely to uncover a large number of abbreviated nursery school programs run for the benefit of church members. In actuality, the number is very, even surprisingly, small.)

Full-time preschool programs tend to enroll a larger proportion of minority children and are much more likely to serve families who receive public assistance (36% versus 17% for part-time programs). When only "educational" preprimary programs are considered, this tendency toward under-representation of minorities in part-time (part-day) programs is confirmed at the national level.[17] Full-time preschool programs also enroll more children, on the average, than part-time programs (46 versus 38 children per program).

Casting a Broad Net: What Services Are Provided?

Information about the services provided by church-housed child day care centers is presented in Table 4; detailed results for sub-sample con-

[17] Chorvinsky, op. cit.

Table 4

What Services Are Provided?

Findings from the Follow-up Survey for the
Total Sample of Church-Housed Child Day Care Centers
(Total Sample Size = 1,506)

Question/Variable	Responses	Total *Number* of Centers Responding
6. The percentage of centers offering each type of program:		*1,506*
a. Infant program (birth to 2 yr)	29.0%	
b. Toddler program (1½ to 3 yr)	45.2%	
c. Preschool program (3 to 5 yr)	94.8%	
d. Before/after school program	28.5%	
e. Mother's program	27.6%	
f. Care of handicapped children	63.6%	
7. Infant programs—time of operation:		
a. Hours per week		*432*
15 or fewer	22.2%	
16-29	6.3%	
30-44	8.8%	
45 or more	62.7%	
b. Days per week		*435*
1-4	33.3%	
5	66.0%	
6-7	0.7%	
c. Months per year		*437*
1-8	1.1%	
9-10	25.2%	
11-12	73.7%	
8. Toddler program—time of operation:		
a. Hours per week		*674*
15 or fewer	16.9%	
16-29	6.5%	
30-44	9.6%	
45 or more	66.9%	
b. Days per week		*678*
1-4	31.3%	
5	68.4%	
6-7	0.3%	
c. Months per year		*680*
1-8	1.0%	
9-10	27.2%	
11-12	71.8%	

Table 4—continued

Question/Variable	Responses	Total *Number* of Centers Responding
9. Preschool program—time of operation:		
a. Hours per week		*1,413*
15 or fewer	14.1%	
16-29	6.7%	
30-44	11.6%	
45 or more	67.6%	
b. Days per week		*1,417*
1-4	24.1%	
5	75.7%	
6-7	0.1%	
c. Months per year		*1,428*
1-8	4.0%	
9-10	51.1%	
11-12	44.9%	
10. Special services provided by centers (% offering each service indicated):		*1,506*
a. Referral to other day care	51.5%	
b. Associated family day care	6.1%	
c. Parental counseling	29.3%	
d. Parenting courses	20.4%	
e. Routine health care	14.1%	
f. Sick child care	3.5%	
g. Emergency drop-off care	11.2%	
h. Evening care (after 6:00 p.m.)	0.7%	

trasts are presented in Appendices 3 through 5. Preschool programs for three- and four-year-old children are by far the most prevalent program type, being offered by 95% of the centers surveyed. This finding reflects consumer demand both by working parents and by parents who do not need extended child care but believe that preschool offers important socialization experiences that prepare children to cope more effectively in school. Changes in family size (from larger to smaller), structure (from extended to nuclear), and lifestyle (from neighborhood-centered to home-centered) have deprived many children of opportunities to interact extensively and intensively with other children. For such children and families, preschool experience becomes a vital dimension of growing up.

The reader is reminded that multiple programs located in the same church building generally operate more or less indistinguishably from one another under a single administrative umbrella. It is particularly important when interpreting findings about care of disabled children to realize that the vast majority of these "program offerings" are not distinct from programs for non-disabled children. Furthermore, the percent of programs *offering* care for disabled children does not necessarily represent the percent of programs actually *enrolling* disabled children. Program directors were asked, "May children with special needs participate in your program?"—not "Do they participate?" Nevertheless, the apparent willingness of church-housed child day care centers to serve disabled children—64% responded that children with special needs "may" participate—should be noted and possibly "exploited" by agencies seeking placements for children with special needs who otherwise might be isolated from their peers during the critical period of early childhood.

Other program types are offered at a minority of centers: toddler programs at 45%; infant, before/after school, and mothers' support programs at 28% through 29%.

The times of day, week, and year that a program operates may be its most important features in the eyes of parents seeking regular and extended child care that meshes with their own work schedules. However, it should not be assumed that programs operating for less than nine hours per day, five days per week, or twelve months per year are useless to working parents. On the contrary, many parents design rather complicated child care "packages"—including everything from in-home babysitters to part-day preschool programs that are explicitly educational—to meet their needs for full-time child care. Not infrequently, parents devise such complicated packages by choice rather than necessity. Thus, it should not be inferred that only full-time programs serve working parents.

There is a common perception, frequently communicated to staff of the Child Day Care Project as they designed the study, that the majority of programs housed in churches operate on abbreviated, part-day schedules in the fashion of traditional nursery schools. In fact, the majority of programs—infant, toddler, and preschool—operate for 45 or more hours per week and five days per week.[18] Moreover, the majority of infant and toddler programs are also open for 11 to 12 months per year. Preschool programs are more likely to follow the school year: 51% are open for nine to ten months; 45% for eleven to twelve months.

Some centers also offer special services to families. For example, a majority (52%) refer parents to other day care in the community as necessary. Smaller numbers provide other services ranging from parental

[18] When reporting how many hours per week programs operate, for split-session programs, we report only the hours per week per "part-day session."

counseling (29%) to routine health care (14%), and a much smaller number (1%) offer evening care after 6:00 p.m.

Church-Operated Versus Independently Operated Centers

Church-operated centers are somewhat more likely (99% versus 95%) to offer preschool programs and are somewhat less prepared (60% versus 67%) to enroll disabled children than are independently operated centers. Regarding preparedness or willingness to enroll disabled children, the difference seems especially small when contributing factors are considered. As discussed later in this chapter, independently operated centers rely more heavily on public funding through various government programs than do church-operated centers. The regulations of these programs often require that space be made available to children with disabling conditions. Although church-operated programs are less likely to be governed by such regulations or to receive special subsidies for offering services, they are only slightly less prepared to enroll disabled children. How many programs of whatever type *actually* serve disabled children is not known.

No differences were found in the hours per week that the two types of centers operated. However, both toddler and preschool programs are open for more months per year, on the average, in independently operated than in church-operated centers, and toddler programs tend to be open more days per week in independently operated centers. Also, independently operated centers are somewhat more likely to offer additional services: associated family day care (8% versus 5%), routine health care (20% versus 10%), and emergency drop-off care (14% versus 9%). As has been suggested, some of these services may be required and subsidized by public monies, which more frequently fund independently operated programs.

As observed in the preceding section, church-operated centers seem less likely to serve low-income families than do independently operated centers. Observed differences in the services offered may largely reflect the responsiveness of church-operated programs to the parents they serve, who probably have fewer needs for emergency care, routine health care, and perhaps even programs with extended operating times.

For-Profit Versus Non-Profit Centers

Non-profit centers are more likely than for-profit centers to offer infant (31% versus 22%), toddler (49% versus 38%), and mothers' support (30% versus 19%) programs. For-profits are more likely (100%

versus 96%) to offer preschool programs. However, when for-profits provide infant care, they are far more likely than non-profits (92% versus 66%) to offer care for at least five days per week, and when they provide toddler care, they are more likely to operate for 45 or more hours per week (86% versus 67%). Non-profits, however, tend to operate preschool programs for more months per year. Regarding additional services, the only statistically significant difference involves emergency drop-off care: for-profits are more likely to provide it (19% versus 11%).

If one believes that the characteristics of for-profit centers are largely the product of market forces, these findings suggest that (1) demand and/or profit is greatest in the area of preschool programming, (2) infant and toddler programs are more economically viable if they provide full-time care, probably to working parents, (3) preschool programs are sufficiently attractive to non-working as well as working parents that they need not offer year-round care to be marketable, and (4) there is additional profit to be had from allowing emergency drop-off, probably at hourly rates significantly higher than those charged for regular service. These speculations are intended to describe rather than evaluate or judge for-profit centers. Indeed, for-profits may well offer the most reliable index we have of current child day care needs in our rapidly changing society, at least among the families in the nation who purchase child care services.

Part-time Versus Full-time Preschool Programs

Most of the variables considered in Table 4 (i.e., 6–8) are not relevant to comparisons of part-time with full-time preschool programs. Variable 9a—hours per week of operation—was used to define part-time versus full-time preschool, but is of interest because the distribution of responses reveals that the majority (68%) of part-time programs are quite abbreviated, operating for 15 or fewer hours per week, while most (85%) of programs defined as full-time operate for 45 or more hours per week. In short, most programs either provide something approaching full-time child care or offer part-day programs that are clearly not intended to provide comprehensive child care for parents working full time. Within the total sample, 68% of programs fall in the former category; only 14%, in the latter. It is not surprising in light of the definition used here that full-time programs are much more likely than part-time programs to operate for five days per week (85% versus 41%). They are also more likely to be open for 11 or 12 months per year (53% versus 15%).

In keeping with the concern that full-time programs have for providing full-time care, they are also more likely to refer parents to other day care, to operate associated family day care, and to accept children on an emergency drop-off basis.

Reflections on Purpose: What Are the Goals of Church-Housed Programs?

Table 5 presents the distribution of responses by program directors to a request that they "check THREE purposes (and only THREE for each age group) which best describe your program's approach." Table 5 also presents the rank orders of goals, reflecting their relative importance from highest (1) to lowest (10). Detailed results for sub-sample contrasts are presented in Appendices 3 through 5.

Responses to this item seem likely to represent a synthesis of directors' personal objectives with their perceptions of what parents expect their programs to accomplish. Predictably and reasonably, a small number of respondents (10%) rebelled and checked more than three alternatives. Nevertheless, the pattern of responses that emerged appears plausible and interpretable.

Far and away the most important goals of the infant programs surveyed are to provide love and warmth (selected by 87%) and to provide basic child care for working parents (82%). These goals remain important (ranked 1 or 2) in programs for older children, with the exception of child care for working parents, which was selected for only 31% of preschool programs, dropping it to fifth rank among the ten goals listed. If one assumes that programs are in most respects responsive to their clientele, this finding suggests that the reasons for preschool enrollment have less to do with parental necessity related to work or other factors than have the reasons for enrollment at other ages. Interestingly, child care for working parents rebounds to first place among before/after school programs, having been selected by 68% of directors.

Other goals that rank among the top three on one or more occasions are independence/self-reliance, positive self-image, and sharing/cooperation. While preparation for school never ranks higher than seventh place, it is most popular among preschool programs (21%), which care for children during the year or two before they enter kindergarten. A similar pattern appears for normal cognitive development, selected by 29% of preschool programs. Concern for children's spiritual development increases gradually through preschool, but never ranks higher than seventh place.

Table 5

What Are the Goals of Church-Housed Programs?

Findings from the Follow-up Survey for the Total Sample of Church-Housed Child Day Care Centers (Total Sample Size = 1,506)

Part A:

Question/Variable	Percent Choosing Each Goal as One of Three Most Important for Particular Program Type			
	11. Infant Program	12. Toddler Program	13. Preschool Program	14. Before/After School Program
11-14. Program Goals				
a. Spiritual development	6.5%	9.8%	15.5%	14.1%
b. Appreciation of own culture	2.5%	3.7%	4.2%	7.4%
c. Provision of love and warmth	86.8%	76.8%	57.2%	63.9%
d. Child care for working parents	81.6%	60.5%	31.4%	68.2%
e. Obedience, manners, discipline	7.5%	9.5%	9.0%	16.2%
f. Preparation for school	1.7%	3.8%	21.0%	8.5%
g. Independence, self-reliance	22.4%	35.8%	40.4%	39.5%
h. Positive self-image	36.1%	36.0%	41.7%	27.6%
i. Sharing, cooperation	30.3%	44.7%	48.4%	36.6%
j. Normal cognitive development	10.9%	14.0%	28.7%	12.0%
Total *Number* Responding:	*402*	*600*	*1,249*	*377*

Part B:

Question/Variable	Goals Rank-Ordered by Importance (1 = highest; 10 = lowest)[a]			
	11. Infant Program	12. Toddler Program	13. Preschool Program	14. Before/After School Program
11-14. Program Goals				
a. Spiritual development	8	7.5	8	7
b. Appreciation of own culture	9	9.5	10	10
c. Provision of love and warmth	1	1	1	2
d. Child care for working parents	2	2	5	1
e. Obedience, manners, discipline	7	7.5	9	6
f. Preparation for school	10	9.5	7	9
g. Independence, self-reliance	5	4.5	4	3
h. Positive self-image	3	4.5	3	5
i. Sharing, cooperation	4	3	2	4
j. Normal cognitive development	6	6	6	8

[a]Percents differing by less than 1.0 are treated as ties.

Church-Operated Versus Independently Operated Centers

The pattern of findings suggests that church-operated centers, more than independently operated centers, have a persistent concern with providing love and warmth and an increasing concern with spiritual development from infancy (5%) through preschool (22%), dropping (to 19%) for before/after school programs. In contrast, independently operated centers exhibit more concern with normal cognitive development through the toddler period, shifting to concern with preparation for school along with the promotion of self-reliance and independence during the preschool years. Independently operated centers are also more likely to operate preschool programs to relieve parents for work or other activities.

For-Profit Versus Non-Profit Centers

Given the small number of for-profit infant (22), toddler (39), and before/after school (33) programs in the study sample, sweeping generalizations from this study to for-profits at large should be avoided. Nevertheless, a striking and rather puzzling finding related to infant program goals seems worth mentioning: 32% (7 of 22) of for-profit infant programs, but only 7% of non-profit infant programs, selected "obedience, manners, discipline" as a major program goal. The full goal description in the questionnare was "to help children be obedient, to accept discipline, to improve manners, and be accepting of adult supervision and control." Whether this situation reflects developmentally unreasonable expectations on the part of for-profit caregivers, or simply a practical concern for toilet training and a modicum of social order in infant programs, is not known.

The findings for preschool programs are straightforward but interesting. Non-profit preschool programs are more concerned with spiritual development, providing love and warmth, and relieving parents for work or other activities. For-profit programs exhibit greater concern with obedience/manners/discipline and preparation for school. Again, the different character of for-profits may simply reflect consumer attitudes and demands.

Finally, non-profit centers place greater emphasis on providing love and warmth in before/after school programs, while for-profits place greater emphasis on normal cognitive development.

Part-time Versus Full-time Preschool Programs

Part-time preschool programs are more concerned with fostering sharing and cooperation; full-time programs, with relieving parents for work. Surprisingly, full-time programs also place greater importance on preparing children for school, belying the commonly held view that full-time day care for preschoolers is basically custodial. Possibly they are more concerned with school preparation because the parents they serve are more concerned and/or because full-time day care providers feel a greater "parenting" responsibility. It is also possible that the children enrolled in full-time day care are at greater risk of not being adequately prepared for school. It is not known whether full-time programs do systematically different things than part-time programs to prepare children for school or whether they are any more successful in the preparation.

The Adults in Child Care: Who Provides Child Care Services?

Table 6 presents what was discovered about those who care for children in church-housed programs; detailed results for sub-sample contrasts are presented in Appendices 3 through 5.

Limitations in the questionnaire and resulting misunderstandings on the part of respondents made it necessary to disregard numerous responses to questions about staff education and training. Thus, the total number of responses considered for variables 15 through 17 is smaller than desirable. Question 18—religious screening—speaks to the characteristics of child care staff by implication only. Questions 19 and 20 consider persons, other than paid staff, who may assume some program responsibilities.

On the whole, directors of church-housed programs are quite well educated. Fully 87% have college degrees, and 25% of these have post-graduate degrees of some sort. Teachers in church-housed programs are also generally well educated: 74% have college degrees; 8% of these have post-graduate degrees. These levels of educational qualification seem substantially higher than is characteristic of child day care directors and teachers nationally,[19] though direct comparisons cannot be made. Pre-

---

[19]Coelen, Glantz, & Calore, op. cit.

Table 6

Who Provides Child Care Services?
Findings from the Follow-up Survey for the
Total Sample of Church-Housed Child Day Care Centers
(Total Sample Size = 1,506)

Question/Variable	Responses	Total *Number* of Centers Responding
15. What is the highest level of education attained by the center's director?		*1,145*
postgraduate degree	25.0%	
college undergraduate degree	62.0%	
high school diploma/equivalent	13.0%	
16. What level of educational attainment best describes the center's teachers as a group?		*912*
postgraduate degree	7.6%	
college undergraduate degree	66.8%	
high school diploma/equivalent	25.7%	
17. What level of educational attainment best describes the center's teacher aides as a group?		*808*
postgraduate degree	1.1%	
college undergraduate degree	17.7%	
high school diploma/equivalent	81.2%	
18. How important are religious beliefs in staff selection?		*1,404*
very important	18.2%	
somewhat important	29.2%	
of little importance	14.7%	
not at all important	37.8%	
19. Do volunteers from community groups help to provide service?		*1,407*
yes	60.4%	
no	39.6%	
20. In what ways do parents help out?		*1,506*
a. Work regularly with teacher	25.6%	
b. Help with field trips	74.6%	
c. Provide occasional snacks	66.4%	

dictably, teacher aides are much less likely than directors and teachers to have college degrees.

The religious beliefs of applicants are given some consideration in the hiring decisions of 62% of centers, though only 18% consider religious beliefs to be "very important" in staff selection. This generally moderate level of concern about the religious beliefs of prospective staff among independently operated as well as church-operated centers may represent concern about the appropriateness of the social models that adults provide children rather than concern about theological orientation. The fact that concern is moderate also provides further evidence that the churches operating child care programs do not see their purpose primarily in terms of Christian education.

The majority of church-housed programs draw upon various services from volunteers in addition to the services of their regular staff. Sixty percent of programs receive some help from volunteers associated with community groups, and a majority rely upon parents to help out in one or more ways—working regularly with teachers (26%), helping with field trips (75%), and providing occasional snacks (66%). Whether volunteer contributions significantly reduce the level of investment that programs must make in paid staff is not known.

Church-Operated Versus Independently Operated Centers

The staffs of church-operated and independently operated centers do not differ with respect to formal educational background. However, 78% of church-operated centers, but only 39% of independently operated centers, give some consideration to religious beliefs in hiring staff. This suggests that church-operated center staff are more likely to be professed Christians. It is interesting that so many independently operated church-housed centers pay any attention to the religious beliefs of staff. This may very well indicate that these programs, presently perceived by pastors as "independent" of the church, were once more closely tied to the churches in which they are housed and perhaps still share basic values with the congregations where they operate. This finding merely reinforces the point made in the introduction to this chapter: the distinction between "church-operated" and "independently operated" centers is often difficult to make. Information from telephone interviews, site visits, and regional conferences of church-housed providers further indicates that many independent programs are *informally* tied to the churches by the religious sentiments of staff and by staff membership in the congregation.

For-Profit Versus Non-Profit Centers

For-profit and non-profit centers do not differ with respect to the educational levels of their staffs. However, non-profits are more likely than for-profits (64% versus 44%) to consider religious beliefs when hiring. This finding may be explained by the fact that the majority of non-profit centers are church-operated.

It was somewhat surprising to find that compared with for-profit centers, non-profit centers do not make significantly more use of volunteers from community groups. Perhaps a more refined measure of the magnitude of contributions by volunteers would reveal differences. As for parental contributions, parents are more likely to work regularly with teachers in non-profit centers (27%) than in for-profit centers (14%).

Part-time Versus Full-time Preschool Programs

As with the previous two contrasts, no differences were found in staff education. Moreover, part-time and full-time preschool programs do not differ with respect to the importance they attach to the religious beliefs of staff. However, full-time preschool programs are more likely (62% versus 55%) to receive help from volunteers associated with community groups, while parents are more likely (35% versus 23%) to work regularly with teachers in part-time programs.

The Pursuit of Excellence: What Can Be Said About Program Quality?

Quality is an elusive concept, residing ultimately in the "eye of the beholder." Most of the programs that Child Day Care Project staff have come to know through firsthand experience in the wake of this survey have exhibited substantial quality as measured by the responsiveness of these programs to the needs of their clients and of the larger community. Having said this, however, we must gain whatever perspective is possible on church-housed programs in relation to currently popular standards of quality that influence decision-making and programming within the day care community at large—postponing more philosophical considerations of quality until the Epilogue.

The most widely acknowledged yardsticks for assessing quality are the findings and recommendations of the National Day Care Study.[20] One

---

[20] Administration for Children, Youth and Families. *Children at the center: Executive summary* (Final report of the National Day Care Study). Cambridge, MA: Abt Associates, Inc., 1979.

facet of the study involved a national survey of day care centers drawn almost entirely from state licensing lists;[21] a second facet involved in-depth studies of a small number of day care centers chosen nonrandomly to represent variations of particular interest.[22] All centers studied by the NDCS operated for at least 25 hours per week and nine months per year, and virtually all were licensed. Thus, neither the national sample nor the in-depth study sample of the NDCS is comparable to the sample of church-housed centers considered here—a significant number of which are non-licensed and operate for less than 25 hours per week and nine months per year. Nevertheless, the NDCS findings offer important points of reference that cannot be neglected by any contemporary study of child day care.

The in-depth study of the NDCS provided the major insights into issues of quality considered here. It was mainly concerned with identifying features of child day care centers that might be regulated through licensing to produce higher quality care and more favorable outcomes among children. Quality was measured in terms of children's development and the character of child and adult behavior in the day care setting. When various features of day care center operations and staffing were correlated with outcomes representing quality, several important quality indicators were identified, for both preschool and infant/toddler programs:

- *Caregiver qualifications*: Caregivers with more education/training relevant to young children tend to provide higher quality care. This relationship is strongest in programs for preschool-age children.[23]
- *Staff/child ratio*: When individual staff members are responsible for smaller numbers of children, quality of care tends to be higher. This finding is strong for infant/toddler programs, but weak and inconsistent for preschool programs.[24]
- *Group size*: Smaller groupings of children are consistently associated with higher quality care in infant/toddler and preschool programs. Among preschool programs, group size is clearly the best predictor of both positive behaviors in the day care setting and child development.[25]

---

[21] Coelen, Glantz, & Calore, op. cit.

[22] Ruopp, Travers, Glantz, & Coelen, op. cit.

[23] Administration for Children, Youth and Families, op. cit., pp. 3-4.

[24] Ibid.

[25] Ibid., p. 2.

The report goes on to say that adequate quality can be achieved in preschool programs if group size does not exceed 18 children *and* the number of children per caregiver does not exceed 9. Although the conditions necessary for achieving quality in infant/toddler programs were not clearly indicated by NDCS findings, the authors also make these recommendations: that a single adult care for no more than 4 infants/toddlers (or 5 on an enrollment basis) and that group size be no more than 8–12 for infants and 12 for toddlers.[26]

NDCS findings and recommendations certainly do not represent the "last word" regarding quality of child care. Indeed, NDCS recommendations of particular maximum staff/child ratios and group sizes in infant and toddler programs appear to lack any solid basis in research findings. Nevertheless, the NDCS study has significantly raised public consciousness about the issue of quality day care and offers a well-known point of reference for placing church-housed programs in perspective.

Thus, an effort was made to develop comparable, *though not identical*, measures of group size, staff/child ratio, and early childhood education/training from responses to the follow-up survey of church-housed centers. These characteristics of staff and programs are described for the total sample of centers in Tables 7 and 8. Detailed results for sub-sample contrasts are presented in Appendices 3 through 5.

With respect to the extent of education/training specifically relevant to early childhood, the follow-up survey shows that most (87%) of program directors in the sample have had some such education/training, and nearly all centers (91%) have at least one teacher on staff who has received such education/training. Formal training or education related to early childhood or child development is much less prevalent among teacher aides—only 69% of centers employ aides with such experience.

The follow-up questionnaire provided more precise and informative data regarding staff/child ratios and group size. Although the response categories used in asking about staff/child ratios make direct comparisons with NDCS results imprecise, it can be seen in Table 8 that a majority of infant and preschool programs comply with NDCS recommendations for staff/child ratio but that a majority of toddler programs do not. The situation in church-housed toddler programs, however, is quite similar to the situation in the day care centers investigated by the NDCS, where they found staff/child ratios in toddler programs to average 1 adult to 5.9 children.[27] Since findings from the NDCS did not clearly indicate that staff/child ratios of 1:4 are necessary to achieve quality care in toddler

---

[26] Ibid., pp. 25-27.

[27] Ruopp, Travers, Glantz, & Coelen, op. cit., p. 264.

Table 7
What Can Be Said About Program Quality?—I
Findings from the Follow-up Survey for the
Total Sample of Church-Housed Child Day Care Centers
(Total Sample Size = 1,506)

Question/Variable	Responses	Total *Number* of Centers Responding
21. Has the center's director had any education or formal training in early childhood/child development?		*1,367*
yes	86.9%	
no	13.1%	
22. Have any teachers had education or formal training in early child-hood/child development?		*1,374*
yes	91.3%	
no	8.7%	
23. Have any teacher aides had educa-tion or formal training in early childhood/child development?		*1,025*
yes	69.0%	
no	31.0%	

programs, perhaps the NDCS recommendation should be reconsidered. Findings from this study and the NDCS indicate that the providers of child day care have found it feasible to work with larger numbers of toddlers than infants, and larger numbers of preschoolers than toddlers, at one time. Child development theory and common sense would also suggest that one adult can adequately care for more older than younger children at one time. Thus, we would not be surprised if more thorough research revealed that quality care can be achieved in toddler programs by maintaining staff/child ratios that fall somewhere between the 1:4 ratio recommended for infant programs and the 1:9 maximum recommended for preschool programs.

Group sizes among church-housed programs seem generally in line with NDCS findings and recommendations. The mean group size for church-housed infant programs is 8.7, compared with the NDCS finding of 8.9 among infant programs nationally and an NDCS recommendation

Table 8
What Can Be Said About Program Quality?—II
Findings from the Follow-up Survey for the
Total Sample of Church-Housed Child Day Care Centers
(Total Sample Size = 1,506)

Question/Variable	Percent of Responses in Each Category by Program Type		
	24a. Infant Program	24b. Toddler Program	24c. Preschool Program
24. What is the approximate staff/child ratio at 11:00 a.m., considering only staff working directly with children?			
1 adult to 2 children	9.6%	3.3%	2.1%
1 adult to 3-4 children	51.9%	22.4%	5.4%
1 adult to 5-6 children	31.1%	36.0%	18.6%
1 adult to 7-8 children	5.4%	22.8%	32.4%
1 adult to 9-10 children	1.9%	12.7%	25.7%
1 adult to 11-15 children	.2%	2.3%	13.7%
1 adult to 16 or more	—	0.6%	2.1%
Total *Number* Responding	*428*	*662*	*1,399*
25. What is the average group or class size?			
fewer than 6 children	30.2%	14.1%	4.0%
6-9 children	35.6%	27.8%	14.7%
10-18 children	28.2%	49.7%	60.9%
19-22 children	1.2%	3.8%	10.1%
more than 22 children	4.7%	4.6%	10.3%
Total *Number* Responding	*404*	*630*	*1,230*
[Mean group size]	[8.72]	[10.88]	[14.84]

of 8 to 12 infants per group.[28] The mean group size for church-housed toddler programs is 10.9, well below the NDCS finding of 12.8 toddlers per group nationally[29] and an NDCS recommended level of 12 toddlers per group. Finally, the mean group size for church-housed preschool programs is 14.8, compared with NDCS findings of 14.3 four-year-olds and 13.9 three-year-olds per group on the average nationally and an NDCS recommended level of 18 or fewer preschoolers per group. Fully 80% of church-housed preschool programs fall within recommended levels. It should be remembered that group size was the most consistent predictor of quality identified by the NDCS across all program levels.

[28] Coelen, Glantz, & Calore, op. cit., p. 117.

[29] Ibid.

By comparison with the yardsticks of quality recommended by the NDCS, church-housed programs measure up rather well and, in this respect, are quite like child day care programs in the nation at large.

Another practical index of quality, which is often used by government in allocating program subsidies and by parents in selecting programs for their children, is licensing status. Although licensing standards vary considerably from state to state, licensed centers can be assumed to have met certain minimum standards thought to ensure children's safety and general well-being. The follow-up questionnaire to church-housed centers asked which programs were licensed. Unfortunately because of errors in coding, this information could not be entered into the computer data files used in the analyses reported here. However, responses were re-tallied by hand for the total sample of centers, though not for each contrast. The percent of licensed programs of each type is given here rather than in the tables: infant programs, 63%; toddler programs, 68%; preschool programs, 70%; and before/after school programs, 82%. Only 16% of centers reported having no programs that were licensed.

While all states, at the time of the survey, had in force some licensing procedures and regulations governing at least some early childhood programs, not all states had licensing procedures for all of the types of programs surveyed by the Child Day Care Project. The generally high percentage of licensed programs among church-housed centers would be even higher if programs that *could not* have been licensed, simply because of the states in which they operated, had been excluded from the analysis. For example, an infant care program operating in New Jersey would have been classified as unlicensed simply because the state did not have licensing procedures in effect at that time for infant programs.

In addition, a number of states exempt church programs from licensing requirements. While many church-operated programs are in voluntary compliance with licensing regulations in these states, those without licenses appear among the ranks of unlicensed programs. The number of states exempting church-operated programs from licensing requirements is growing. This specific issue of licensing is considered further in the Epilogue.

Church-Operated Versus Independently Operated Centers

Independently operated centers are somewhat more likely than church-operated centers to have teachers (94% versus 91%) and aides (75% versus 66%) on staff with some formal training/education in early childhood or child development. Independently operated centers are also likely to have more favorable staff/child ratios at the infant level and particularly the preschool level, where 66% of independently operated centers, but only 53% of church-operated centers, have ratios more favorable than 1 to 9. No difference was found in the most important of the three proposed indices of quality—group size.

The findings of difference in staff/child ratio favoring independently operated infant and preschool programs were particularly disconcerting to staff of the Child Day Care Project. Although staff/child ratios are not predictive of child development outcomes, according to the NDCS, these ratios are correlated with various aspects of children's day-to-day experience in the day care setting—dimensions of experience, such as one-to-one interaction with the caregiver, that many early childhood experts, parents, and readers of this book would likely associate with general quality of care. No fully satisfactory explanation of this difference was found in the information available to the study or in hypothesis. Its meaning and implications are considered further in the Epilogue.

For-Profit Versus Non-Profit Centers

Only one difference was found with respect to program quality indicators: for-profit centers maintain smaller average group sizes in infant programs than do non-profit centers. We found this somewhat surprising because discussion of for-profit day care, among child care experts and advocates, is so often critical of program quality. Although one cannot confidently generalize from our small and potentially unrepresentative sample to for-profit centers at large, the apparent success of for-profit day care in maintaining basic standards of program quality should give critics pause.

Part-time Versus Full-time Preschool Programs

Full-time preschool programs are more likely to have at least one teacher with some education/training related to early childhood. Part-time preschool programs tend to have both more favorable staff/child ratios and smaller group sizes. The latter finding, which suggests the possibility of more individualized attention in part-time programs, lends some credence to common perceptions that full-time programs tend to offer more basic, essentially custodial care. Undoubtedly, the necessity of keeping program costs in line with what parents can afford and/or what governmental agencies pay in subsidies encourages centers to control their single greatest expense—staff costs. However, fuller explanation of apparent differences in staff/child ratio and group size awaits further research.

Provider or Landlord: How Are Programs Administered?

Information about program administration is presented in Table 9; detailed results for sub-sample contrasts are presented in Appendices 3 through 5.

Infant programs are most likely (61%) to be operated by churches; toddler programs, least likely (56%). Overall, 56% of centers responding to the follow-up questionnaire are church-operated. In spite of this fact, only 28% of centers are directly subject to the policy decisions of church boards, at least from the perspective of center directors, which suggests that even church-operated centers are not tightly controlled by the church. Parents of children enrolled in the center are far more likely (54%) than church boards (28%) to play some formal role in program policy making. Finally, relatively few church-housed centers (10%) are proprietorships—that is, for-profit operations. The percent of church-housed centers that are operated for profit appears to be considerably smaller than the percent of day care centers operated for profit nationally. A national survey of licensed centers conducted in 1976–77 indicated that 41% of these centers were operated for profit.[30] Perhaps churches are less desirable locations for profit-making operations. Very probably, churches are less receptive to housing for-profit programs.

Church-Operated Versus Independently Operated Centers

Church boards more frequently play some formal policy-making role in church-operated centers (41%) than in independently operated centers (10%). Even so, it is surprising that church boards do not have, or are not perceived to have, more direct involvement in programs that are nominally and often legally their responsibility.

Parents are somewhat more likely to take formal policy-making responsibility for independently operated programs (59% versus 52%).

For-Profit Versus Non-Profit Centers

Few for-profit centers are classified as church-operated. Those that are (9%) represent anomalies that cannot be adequately explained using

[30] Ruopp, Travers, Glantz, & Coelen, op. cit.

Table 9
How Are Programs Administered?
Findings from the Follow-up Survey for the
Total Sample of Church-Housed Child Day Care Centers
(Total Sample Size = 1,506)

Question/Variable	Responses	Total *Number* of Centers Responding
26. Is the program operated by the congregation or independently of the congregation under a rental/use agreement?		
a. Infant programs		*397*
church-operated	60.7%	
independently operated	39.3%	
b. Toddler programs		*626*
church-operated	56.1%	
independently operated	43.9%	
c. Preschool programs		*1,269*
church-operated	57.9%	
independently operated	42.1%	
d. Child day care centers—all programs under common administration in the same church		*1,342*
church-operated	56.1%	
independently operated	43.9%	
27. Is the program/center a proprietorship—i.e., operated for profit?		*1,240*
for-profit center	9.6%	
non-profit center	90.4%	
28. Is the church board formally involved in setting program policy?		*1,506*
yes	28.0%	
no	72.0%	
29. Are parents formally involved in setting program policy?		*1,506*
yes	54.1%	
no	45.9%	

available information. Perhaps some of the pastors, in classifying programs, considered for-profit programs, if they were operated by church members, to be operated by the "church or congregation," quite apart from any consideration of formal ties between program and church.

Parents are much more likely to have some formal responsibility for setting program policy in non-profit centers (61%) than in for-profit centers (11%).

Part-time Versus Full-time Preschool Programs

The only finding of difference between part-time and full-time preschool programs was that parents of children in full-time programs are somewhat more likely to play some formal role in setting program policy.

Making Ends Meet: What Are the Sources of Income and the Expenses of Centers?

Information about the income and expenses of church- housed programs is presented in Table 10; detailed results for sub-sample contrasts are presented in Appendices 3 through 5.

The standard fees charged parents of children enrolled in infant and toddler programs are, when rounded to the nearest dollar, the same—an average of $33 per week. Standard weekly fees for preschool programs are about one fifth less—an average of $27. This difference may be explained in part by differences in staff/child ratio (see Table 8, page 57)—one adult being able to care for more preschoolers than infants at one time. A majority of centers make some provision for enrolling children whose parents cannot afford the standard fee: 11% charge on a sliding scale according to the parent's ability to pay; 57% offer scholarships or subsidies.

By far the most common source of income is parents' fees, 94% of centers deriving some income from that source. Next most common are contributions from individuals, reported by 34% of centers. Other sources—including major federal support programs such as Title XX and the Child Care Food Program—were each mentioned by fewer than 25% of centers surveyed. Indeed, cash contributions by churches and religious groups appear to be as prevalent as any government support program. A majority of church-housed centers (64%) rely exclusively upon income from private sources; 34% receive money from both private and public sources; and only 3% rely exclusively on public funding.

Salaries paid to staff represent the major expense of child care programs. Data summarized in Table 10 offer a rough estimate of the wages paid to different categories of staff in 1982. The rates of response to questions about staff wages were low. Moreover, many responses were

Table 10

What Are the Sources of Income and the Expenese of Centers?

Findings from the Follow-up Survey for the
Total Sample of Church-Housed Child Day Care Centers
(Total Sample Size = 1,506)

Question/Variable	Responses	Total *Number* of Centers Responding
30. What is the fee charged to parents per child per week?		
a. Infant programs		*385*
no fee	5.5%	
$10 or less	22.1%	
$11-$25	12.5%	
$26-$40	24.4%	
$41-$55	21.0%	
$56-$85	12.5%	
more than $85	2.1%	
[mean fee]	[$33.01]	
b. Toddler programs		*594*
no fee	3.4%	
$10 or less per week	21.2%	
$11-$25	12.6%	
$26-$40	30.3%	
$41-$55	21.4%	
$56-$85	9.4%	
more than $85	1.7%	
[mean fee]	[$32.94]	
c. Preschool programs		*1,209*
no fee	2.9%	
$10 or less	26.7%	
$11-$25	23.0%	
$26-$40	24.5%	
$41-$55	17.3%	
$56-$85	4.5%	
more than $85	1.1%	
[mean fee]	[$26.83]	
31. Do parents pay a fixed fee or a sliding scale fee?		*1,323*
sliding scale	11.1%	
fixed	88.9%	
32. If parents cannot afford the full cost of care, are subsidies or scholarships offered?		*1,329*
yes	57.3%	
no	42.7%	

Table 10—continued

Question/Variable	Percent	Total *Number* of Centers Responding
33. All sources of program funding during 1981:		*1,351*
a. Parents' fees	93.8%	
b. Title XX	15.1%	
c. Title IV A	8.4%	
d. Child Care Food Programs	22.9%	
e. CETA	9.3%	
f. Other federal government	7.5%	
g. Other state government	7.5%	
h. Other local government	10.3%	
i. Church or religious groups	21.3%	
j. Private voluntary groups	11.5%	
k. Business/industry	5.1%	
l. Individual contributions	34.0%	
34. Reliance on private versus public funding for programs during 1981:		*1,351*
private funding only	63.6%	
private and public funding	33.9%	
public funding only	2.5%	
35. Average monthly wages paid to full-time staff:		
a. Director's monthly wage (mean)	$1,039	*561*
b. Teacher's monthly wage (mean)	$750	*502*
c. Aide's monthly wage (mean)	$615	*251*
36. Are any fringe benefits offered to staff?		*1,350*
yes	56.7%	
no	43.4%	
37. What amount of rent is paid to the church each month?		*1,331*
none	48.5%	
$1-$100	20.7%	
$101-$200	8.3%	
$201-$300	6.5%	
$301-$500	6.6%	
$501-$1,000	5.6%	
more than $1,000	3.9%	
[mean rent paid]	[$142]	

not interpretable. Thus, the small number of responses summarized here may not be representative of church-housed centers as a whole and should be interpreted cautiously. It should also be noted (see Table 4, page 42) that not all programs operate for twelve months of the year and not all programs provide full-time employment even when they are operating. Nevertheless, it is worth considering what the average annual salaries of staff would be, assuming twelve months of employment: $12,486 for a center director; $9,000 for a teacher; and $7,380 for a teacher's aide. By any standard, such annual salaries would be considered modest, particularly since most directors (87%) and teachers (74%) have college degrees (see Table 6, page 51). Nor do fringe benefits appear to compensate for modest wages: only 57% of centers offer any fringe benefits. Since the questionnaire asked, "Do you offer any fringe benefits to your staff in addition to salary?", the percent answering "yes" very probably include some that offer only holiday/vacation/sick-leave benefits rather than medical insurance and retirement benefits, which more clearly represent additional though deferred compensation.

Another major source of expense for child care programs is the cost of indoor/outdoor space for program operation. Average rents paid by church-housed centers are low—$142 per month. Nearly one half (49%) of the centers surveyed pay no rent at all.

Findings from the follow-up survey begin to answer the question, "Who bears the costs of church-housed child day care?" Although available information does not permit direct estimation of the magnitude of contributions from each source identified, there seems little doubt that parents assume the major financial burden. Governmental agencies/programs appear to play relatively minor roles, judged by the low frequency with which particular public support sources were reported. Some part of the expenses incurred by parents is of course recaptured from the federal government in the form of child care tax credits, which represent additional public financing. Information about staff wages and benefits suggests that providers themselves assume significant financial burdens by working for less compensation than would be expected of persons with their generally high educational levels. Among other sources of income and in-kind contribution mentioned, the most important are undoubtedly the host churches. As noted, the monthly rents paid by centers tend to be extremely low, with 49% of centers paying no rent at all. The full scope of church subsidies to child day care programs is examined in the next section of this chapter.

Church-Operated Versus Independently Operated Centers[31]

For infant and toddler programs, church-operated centers charge lower weekly fees than do independently operated centers, whereas fees for preschool programs are virtually identical. Regarding provisions for lower-income families, independently operated centers are more likely to charge on a sliding scale (16% versus 7%), while church-operated centers are more likely to offer scholarships or other subsidies (62% versus 54%).

Church-operated centers more often than independently operated centers (98% versus 91%) mention parents' fees as a source of income; however, parents' fees are the single most important funding source for both types of centers. Independently operated centers are at least twice as likely as church-operated centers to receive funds from the federal and state government sources listed. Seventy-two percent of church-operated centers, but only 54% of independently operated centers, rely exclusively on private funding.

Regarding expenses, the only difference involves rent for indoor/outdoor space—church-operated centers pay substantially lower rent on average ($86 versus $234) than independently operated centers pay. Only 35% of church- operated centers pay any rent at all, whereas 79% of independently operated centers pay some amount of rent to their host churches.

For-Profit Versus Non-Profit Centers

The standard fees charged parents differ only for infant programs, for-profit centers charging more than non-profit centers. However, for-profits are not as accessible to lower-income families, less often employing a sliding scale fee (4% versus 13%) and much less often offering scholarships or other subsidies (31% versus 61%).

Nearly all for-profits and non-profits—95% in both cases—rely on parents' fees for income. However, non-profits have much more diverse sources of funding on the average. Fully 81% of for-profits rely exclusively upon private funding, while only 62% of non-profits rely solely on private sources.

Compared to for-profits, non-profits are much more likely to offer some fringe benefits (59% versus 38%) and to pay lower rents ($136 versus $232).

---

[31] Information about staff wages was not analyzed for this or the other two sub-sample contrasts because low rates of response resulted in very small sub-sample sizes.

Part-time Versus Full-time Preschool Programs

Part-time preschool programs charge much lower fees on the average ($14 per week) than full-time programs charge ($31 per week). Part-time programs are also less likely to charge on a sliding scale, but are just as likely as full- time programs to offer scholarships or other subsidies to allow participation by lower-income families.

Part-time programs have less diverse sources of income. They are no more likely than full-time programs to receive income from any particular source and are less likely to receive income from parents' fees, various federal support programs, private voluntary groups, and individuals. Considering all sources of finance, part-time programs are more likely (81% versus 61%) to rely exclusively on private sources.

Part-time programs are less likely to offer any fringe benefits (44% versus 60%), and they pay much lower monthly rents on the average ($79) than do full-time programs ($160).

Stewardship and Child Care: How Do Churches Contribute to Programs?

Major financial and in-kind contributions to centers from their host churches are described in Table 11; detailed results for sub-sample contrasts are presented in Appendices 3 through 5.

Over one half of the centers surveyed are permitted to use indoor (55%) and outdoor (63%) space free of charge. Only 24% of centers pay market value rent for indoor space; only 19% pay full rent for outdoor space. Nearly three quarters (74%) of centers pay nothing or less than market rates for utilities. Most (81%) pay nothing or less than the full value of building repairs, and only 40% cover the full cost of janitorial services. Repairs or replacement of equipment is the only instance in which a majority of centers (70%) pay the entire cost.

In the preceding chapter it was argued that space, location, and tax-exempt status make churches desirable sites for child day care programs. In light of the findings summarized here, another factor should be added to this list of desirable features—churches tend to be very generous landlords, often charging nothing and seldom charging full market rates for the use of church property and a variety of related services.

About one quarter (26%) of centers also report that the churches in which they are housed offer scholarships or other specific subsidies to lower-income families. Considering all the types of contributions about

Table 11

What Specific Contributions Do Churches Make to Centers?
Findings from the Follow-up Survey for the
Total Sample of Church-Housed Child Day Care Centers
(Total Sample Size = 1,506)

Question/Variable	Responses	Total *Number* of Centers Responding
38. Degree to which churches subsidize programs:		
a. Indoor space		*1,410*
church donates at no charge	54.8%	
church charges below market rate	20.9%	
center pays full rent	24.3%	
b. Outdoor space		*1,333*
church donates at no charge	63.3%	
church charges below market rate	17.3%	
center pays full rent	19.4%	
c. Utilities		*1,367*
church provides at no charge	37.7%	
church charges less than value	36.3%	
center covers entire cost	26.0%	
d. Equipment repair/replacement		*1,363*
church provides at no charge	10.0%	
church charges less than value	19.9%	
center covers entire cost	70.1%	
e. Building repair		*1,331*
church provides at no charge	44.0%	
church charges less than value	36.8%	
center covers entire cost	19.2%	
f. Janitorial services		*1,365*
church provides at no charge	33.8%	
church charges less than value	26.4%	
center covers entire cost	39.9%	
39. Does church provide scholarships or otherwise specifically subsidize participation by children from lower-income families?		*1,506*
yes	25.6%	
no	74.4%	
40. Does the church provide *any* subsidy for program operation or family participation?		*1,506*
yes	93.8%	
no	6.2%	

which center directors were queried, we find that fully 94% of centers receive some subsidy from their host churches to support program operation and/or participation by individual families. Thus, in nearly every instance of church-housed child care, the church involved assumes some financial responsibility and might legitimately be considered a *provider* or *co-provider* of child day care.

Church-Operated Versus Independently Operated Centers

It is not surprising that church-operated centers are more likely than independently operated centers to be subsidized, and more completely subsidized, by the churches in which they are located. Even so, fewer than one half of independently operated centers pay full market value for indoor space, outdoor space, utilities, or building repair. Moreover, 87% of independently operated centers receive some subsidy from their host churches to support program operation and/or participation in the program by lower-income families. There can be little doubt that, by subsidizing both their own and others' programs, local churches make a significant contribution to the availability of affordable child day care in their communities.

For-Profit Versus Non-Profit Centers

It is also not surprising that for-profit centers are much less likely than non-profit centers to receive specific subsidies from the churches in which they are located. Half or more of for-profits pay full market value for indoor space, outdoor space, utilities, equipment repair or replacement, and janitorial services. Few for-profits (5% versus 29% of non-profits) receive church scholarship monies or other direct church subsidies for lower-income families. Yet, nearly all for-profit centers (82%) receive some type of subsidy from the churches in which they are located.

Part-time Versus Full-time Preschool Programs

Part-time preschool programs pay less, on the average, than full-time programs pay for the use of church property and related services, though the differences are not as large as those found between church-operated and independently operated centers or between for-profit and non-profit centers. Part-time and full-time preschool programs are equally likely to receive scholarship monies and other subsidies to support participation by children from lower-income families. And they are equally likely to receive some sort of subsidy from the churches in which they are located.

Living With Others: How Do Church-Housed Providers Relate to Church and Community?

Information about how supportive churches are of the programs they house and how familiar center directors are with local, regional, and national child care/advocacy organizations is summarized in Table 12. Detailed results for sub-sample contrasts are presented in Appendices 3 through 5.

Sixty-five percent of center directors view the churches/congregations where they work as supportive or very supportive of their child care program. Only 11% view the church/congregation as unsupportive or very unsupportive, while 24% assess the relationship as being neutral. Thus, most providers feel welcome in the churches where they work.

Little is known about the relationships that exist among local child care providers or the extent to which child care providers are involved in national membership and advocacy organizations. On several occasions such lack of national organization has worked to the detriment of effective advocacy for child care legislation. The present study sought to gain information about these relationships by asking respondents to indicate the groups and/or organizations with which they were familiar. While no comparable data exist for child care providers as a whole, it appears that directors of church-housed centers are relatively unfamiliar with local, regional, and national child care/advocacy organizations. The best known organization is the National Association for the Education of Young Children or its state affiliates; 61% of directors know of its existence, whether or not they participate. Next most familiar are local groups: local child care resource and referral groups (known by 55%) and local child advocacy or day care groups (known by 40%). Familiarity with other regional and national organizations is low, ranging from 5% to 21%.

Particularly surprising is the finding that about half of all church-housed providers report no knowledge of provider groups/networks that address child day care issues within their local communities. To what extent this unfamiliarity with local groups is due to the non-existence of such groups in many local communities or to the isolation of church-housed providers from local provider networks is not known.

Table 12
How Do Church-Housed Providers Relate to Church and Community?
Findings from the Follow-up Survey for the
Total Sample of Church-Housed Child Day Care Centers
(Total Sample Size = 1,506)

Question/Variable	Responses	Total *Number* of Centers Responding
41. Program director's response to the question, "In your view, how supportive of your program is the church/congregation in which you are housed?":		*1,422*
very supportive	33.0%	
supportive	32.2%	
neutral	23.8%	
unsupportive	7.4%	
very unsupportive	3.6%	
42. Program director's familiarity with organizations concerned with child care and early education:		*1,506*
a. Child Welfare League of America	16.8%	
b. Children's Defense Fund	14.6%	
c. Day Care Council of America	21.4%	
d. Four C's	18.8%	
e. Local child care resource and referral groups	54.6%	
f. Local child advocacy and/or day care groups	40.0%	
g. National Association for the Education of Young Children (or state affiliate)	60.8%	
h. National Black Child Development Institute	5.3%	

Church-Operated Versus Independently Operated Centers

Compared with directors of independently operated centers, directors of church-operated centers are more likely to view the churches/congregations where they work as supportive of their program. Yet, nearly all providers—92% of church-sponsored and 85% of independent providers—appear to feel welcome in the churches where they work.

Regarding familiarity with local, regional, and national child care/ advocacy organizations, the directors of church-operated programs are somewhat less familiar than other directors with all regional and national organizations except the National Association for the Education of Young Children, with which directors from both types of centers are equally familiar. At the local level, church-sponsored providers and independent providers are equally familiar with child care resource and referral groups, but church-sponsored providers are slightly less familiar with child advocacy and/or day care groups. These findings suggest that the directors of church-operated programs are somewhat more isolated from the larger day care community than are their peers in independently operated church-housed centers.

For-Profit Versus Non-Profit Centers

Directors of non-profit centers are more likely than directors of for-profit centers to perceive the church/congregation as supportive of their programs, as well they might be, given the already mentioned differential subsidies that churches offer for-profits versus non-profits. The finding of main interest regarding familiarity with child care/advocacy organizations is that non-profits are more likely to know of local child care resource and referral groups (57% versus 47%) and local child advocacy and/or day care groups (43% versus 31%). This difference may reflect a tendency among for-profits to avoid local provider networks because they are dominated by non-profits whose interests tend more to issues of social policy than to business and who often look rather disdainfully upon "commercial" providers as a group.

Part-time Versus Full-time Preschool Programs

Directors of part-time and full-time preschool programs do not differ in their perceptions of church/congregation supportiveness; most feel welcome in the churches where they work. However, they differ substantially with respect to their familiarity with child care/advocacy organizations at the local, regional, and national levels. Directors of part-time preschool programs are consistently less familiar with such organizations than are directors of full-time programs. Since a majority of the regional and national organizations listed in the questionnaire are particularly concerned with social policy as it affects working, minority, and/or poor parents and their children, it is perhaps understandable that part-time programs—serving fewer children of poor, minority, and working parents—have not heard of these organizations and might not even be motivated to discover such organizations. Indeed, many part-time programs may not even be perceived as "day care," but rather as "preschool" or "mothers' support" programs. Similarly at the local level, part-time programs may find the services and support offered by resource, referral, and advocacy groups to be of little relevance, given the needs and goals of their programs and of the families they tend to serve.

Major Findings from the Follow-up Survey

In the preceding pages of this chapter, we have addressed, if not fully answered, a series of questions about the nature of church-housed child day care. We asked these questions of church-housed child care as a whole and of three pairs of contrasting sub-samples: *church-operated centers* versus *independently operated centers*; *for-profit centers* versus *non-profit centers*; and *part-time preschool programs* versus *full-time preschool programs*.

Here, we sketch profiles of the total sample and the contrasting sub-samples, using broad strokes to capture their most distinctive features. We strongly encourage readers to reach their own conclusions, which may be somewhat different from ours, based on the detailed findings presented in previous sections of this chapter.

Church-Housed Child Day Care as a Whole

Church-housed child care does not exist by virtue of any explicit policy of the collective Church; rather, it has evolved from a confluence of local needs, historical coincidence, and religious conviction—the needs of families within and without local congregations for child day care; the coincidence of churches' tax-exempt status, convenient location, appropriate design, and availability for use during the work week; and religious conviction expressed in the Church's various ministries for children and families. The resulting diversity of child care services reflects the pluralism of the nation's religious and secular life.

How extensive is church-housed child care? There is no doubt that the child care programs housed in America's churches represent a substantial portion of all center-based care available to the nation's families. At a minimum, the 15 denominations that participated in this study house programs that care for several hundred thousand children under five years of age. It is very likely that the nation's churches, collectively, house part- or full-day care for several million children.

What is the role of the church in providing care? About half of child care centers surveyed are perceived by pastors to be operated by the church itself. The other half operate quite independently of church administration. Even in the case of independently operated centers, however, host churches typically provide some direct support for program operations in the form of cash or in-kind contributions. Thus, in one way or another, local churches are significantly involved in the provision of most child care services housed on their property.

What types of services are offered? As is the case nationally, the most common child care services housed in church buildings are programs for preschool-age (three- and four-year-old) children. Ninety-five percent of child day care centers located in churches enroll preschoolers; somewhat less than half provide care for toddlers; and slightly more than one quarter provide care for infants and/or school-age children before and after school. Many centers offer more than one program. The majority of centers surveyed offer extended day care to meet all or most of the child care needs of working parents. In addition, as described in Chapter II, churches house a surprising variety of programs designed to support children and families with special needs—programs providing respite care for parents of severely disabled and terminally ill children, support programs for abused and neglected children and their families, programs that bring the very old and the very young together, seasonal programs with extended operating hours to meet the needs of migrant farm workers, and so on and on.

What can be said of program quality? Judged by such commonly used yardsticks of program quality as staff training, staff-child ratio, and group size, church-housed programs appear to measure-up rather well—as well as and in some ways better than center-based day care at large.

How is church-housed child care financed? Nearly two thirds of church-housed child day care centers rely exclusively on income from private sources; one third receive support from both public and private sources; and a very few rely exclusively on public funds. The primary contributors to most programs appear to be parents who pay fees, staff who work for lower wages than they might command in other employment sectors, and local congregations who, among numerous other contributions, provide space and utilities free of charge or below market value to three quarters of the centers surveyed.

Although the Church did not intend to become a major provider of child day care to the nation's families, it very definitely has through the independent actions of local parishes in response to similar needs of families and common ideas of ministry. It is our hope that the findings of this study will help national agencies of the Church come to a greater appreciation of the vast extent of their involvement in child care. Questions of whether and how the Church might act more deliberately in the area of child day care are taken up in the Epilogue.

Church-Operated Versus Independently Operated Centers

In the initial survey, we asked pastors to classify the programs housed in their churches as either church-operated or independently operated under a rental/use agreement. Their classifications were necessarily somewhat arbitrary in many instances, since the relationships between centers and churches actually form a continuum, ranging from centers that are closely managed by church boards under church incorporation to centers that are completely independent corporate entities merely renting space in church buildings. Nevertheless, even the imprecise distinction made here is informative.

What role does religion play? Guided by their understanding of theology and ministry, churches frequently offer week-day child care as an integral part of their church program. However, symbols, practices, and teachings commonly viewed as "religious" are conspicuously absent from most church-operated programs. Church-operated centers are no more likely than independently operated centers to restrict enrollment to members of the congregation, and both are very unlikely to do so. Church-operated centers are somewhat more likely to be concerned with the "spiritual development of the child" than are independently operated centers, but only a small minority of centers consider this a high priority goal. The single area in which religion figures prominently is staff selection: church-operated centers are much more likely to give some consideration to religious beliefs when hiring staff. Thus, while the staff of church-operated centers are perhaps more likely to be professed Christians and probably more likely to be members of the congregation of the church in which the center is housed, the programs they offer are generally open to the community and not distinctly religious.

What sorts of programs are offered? It is rather commonly believed that the child day care offered by churches comprises mainly nursery/preschool programs operated on abbreviated schedules for church members who do not require full-time child care. Findings from the follow-up survey challenge this view. Church-operated centers are just as likely as independently operated centers to care for infants, toddlers, and school-age children. Most programs in both church-operated and independently operated centers offer full-time child care for parents who require it. And church-operated centers are no more likely than independently operated centers to restrict enrollment to church members.

How are centers financed? Church-operated centers tend to rely less on public funds, somewhat more on parent fees, and substantially more on subsidies from sponsoring churches than do independently operated centers. While independently operated centers more often use sliding scale fees to make programs affordable to lower-income parents, church-operated centers more often provide scholarships.

Who is served? Church-operated centers tend to serve children and families somewhat more like families in their congregations and immediate neighborhoods—that is, typically white and middle class—than do independently operated centers. We have no evidence that this is due to exclusionary policies. Rather, it would seem to reflect the fact that church-operated programs typically originate in response to child care needs among families in the congregation or the immediate neighborhood. In addition, since church-operated centers rely less on public funds for their operation, they are less likely to serve poor children whose participation would be subsidized by such funds. Information obtained from interviews with providers and numerous visits to centers across the country suggests that church-operated centers often become more like independently operated centers over time—gradually serving more diverse families within the local community; eventually turning to various governmental programs for supplemental funds; even, in some instances, becoming independent of the sponsoring church.

What can be said of program quality? Judged by widely used basic indicators of program quality, church-operated centers lag somewhat behind independently operated centers. Specifically, church-operated centers have somewhat less favorable staff/child ratios and are less likely than independently operated centers to have staff with early childhood training. No difference was found with respect to group size, considered to be the most important of the three indicators of quality. Though these indicators provide but a minimal definition of quality care, the observed differences should be a matter of some concern. Why these differences exist is not known. What might be done to address them is a matter for consideration by providers, local parishes, and national church leadership.

Are providers isolated? Providers in church-operated centers are less familiar with most national and local day care and child advocacy organizations than independent providers are, though neither group is particularly well informed.

This last finding reinforces an emerging portrait of church-operated centers as tending to be slightly removed from the secular mainstream of child day care. As suggested above, this tendency toward difference and separation frequently diminishes over time as church-operated centers move from meeting the immediate needs of their congregations to serving the larger community.

For-Profit Versus Non-Profit Centers

Only 10% of church-housed centers operate as businesses on a for-profit basis. We took a special look at for-profit centers not because of their numerical importance but because of the controversy that surrounds them. Within the day care community, which is dominated by non-profit operations, for-profit centers bear the brunt of much criticism. Though information about our small and possibly unrepresentative sample of church-housed for-profits cannot substantiate or refute such criticism, it may help to inform current debates.

How are centers financed? For-profit centers tend to rely heavily or exclusively on parent fees. They receive much less support from host churches and receive public funds less often than non-profit centers do. In spite of these facts, the fees charged by for-profits are higher only for infant programs. There are some indications that for-profit centers get their books to balance by compensating staff at lower levels than non-profits. For example, we know that for-profits are less likely to offer any fringe benefits to staff.

Who is served? For-profit centers are much less likely to serve poor and minority children than non-profit centers are.

What can be said about program quality? Only one difference was found with respect to indicators of program quality: for-profit centers maintain smaller group sizes in infant programs than do non-profit centers. Thus, church-housed for-profit centers do not sacrifice basic standards of quality in pursuit of economic goals.

Are providers isolated? For-profit providers are generally less familiar than non-profit providers with both local and national day care and child advocacy organizations.

Information gleaned from the follow-up survey does not suggest that the for-profit child day care centers located in churches are in any respect less adequate than the non- profit centers in our sample. The fact that for-profit centers serve mainly those who can afford to pay comes as no surprise. The fact that for-profit centers do not sacrifice basic standards of quality—indeed, that the only significant difference with respect to quality indicators favored for-profits—may surprise some readers. Finally, the relative isolation of for-profits from the larger day care community possibly reflects their rather different needs for information and support. It may also be their reaction to prevailing negative attitudes toward for-profit centers among other providers and advocates.

Part-time Versus Full-time Preschool Programs

It is our strong impression that part-day nursery/preschool programs constitute a decreasing fraction of the total child care market. As more women enter the work force, full-day programs simply become the more practical alternative. Nevertheless, a significant number of part-day programs have survived the rapidly changing lifestyle of the nation and will probably continue to survive in many places where there are families for whom preschool child care is a preference rather than a necessity.

Initially we examined these abbreviated programs because we were repeatedly advised that they were the predominant form of church-operated program. They are not. Indeed, independently operated centers are just as likely, or unlikely, as church-operated centers to offer part-day preschool programs. However, we continued to be interested in part-day programs because of the widely held opinion that these programs, with no pretense of offering full-time child care, are quite different from full-day care programs.

For purposes of this study we divided our sample of preschool programs into two groups: those operating for less than 30 hours per week—designated *part-time*; those operating for 30 or more hours per week—designated *full-time*. In fact, the contrast is more extreme than this definition suggests. The majority of part-time preschool programs operate for 15 or fewer hours per week, while most full-time programs operate for 45 or more hours per week. Twenty-one percent of church-housed preschool programs are part-time; 79% are full-time. Although some working parents use part-time programs for part of full-time child care, full-time programs are generally more convenient and more often utilized for this purpose.

What are the program's goals? Part-time providers more often select "sharing and cooperation" among children as one of their three most important goals, while full-time providers more often select "basic care" (to relieve working parents) and "preparation for school." However, these statistical findings make part- and full-time preschool programs seem more different than perhaps they are. The only one of these goals that is given high priority by both groups of providers is "sharing and cooperation" (ranked in first place by part-time providers and in second place by full-time providers). There is a slight difference in emphasis on preparing children for school, which may well reflect a legitimate lack of concern for the future school success of the predominantly middle-class children enrolled in part-time programs.

How are programs financed? Part-time preschool programs are more likely than full-time programs to rely exclusively on private funding; yet, they are less likely to collect fees from parents. Since no compensating alternative source of private funds is apparent, we surmise that some number of part-time programs are rather informal, perhaps operating on a volunteer or coop basis. We know, for example, that parent volunteers are more likely to work regularly with teachers in part-time preschool programs. In addition, we know that part-time programs are more likely to have rent and essential services subsidized by the churches in which they are located, not because they are more frequently sponsored by the church, but perhaps because they make fewer demands on church resources and are generally less obtrusive.

Who is served? Part-time preschool programs are much less likely to enroll poor and minority children than are full-time programs. Furthermore, part-time programs are more likely to restrict enrollment to members of the church in which they are located (4.4% versus less than 1%). The meaning of this finding is not clear. Either we have finally managed to locate the elusive "part-time religious nursery school" or we have simply stumbled upon part-time programs that represent informal solutions to child care needs among like-minded parents of a local parish.

What can be said of program quality? Part-time and full-time preschool programs differ with respect to all three indicators of quality. Full-time programs are somewhat more likely to employ teachers who have early childhood training. Part-time programs tend to have more favorable staff/child ratios and to maintain smaller group sizes. Because of the difficulty of making full-time care affordable, findings related to staff/child ratio are hardly surprising. The implication of this and other findings for children is not known.

Are providers isolated? The providers of part-time preschool programs are less familiar than full-time providers with both national and local day care and child advocacy organizations. This situation is not surprising. Major national organizations concerned with day care and child advocacy, and local referral and advocacy groups, tend to be preoccupied with the plight of poor and/or working parents and their children. Part-time providers are less likely than full-time providers to share this preoccupation, given the types of families they predominantly serve.

In short, part- and full-time preschool programs are somewhat different from one another in most respects. It seems to us that these differences mainly reflect differences in the characteristics and needs of the families and children served.

In the next chapter we present first-person accounts in the form of center directors' responses to three "discussion" questions from the follow-up questionnaire. These quotations breathe life into the subject of our study, representing the human experience of child day care in a way that statistics cannot.

IV
The Voices of Providers: An Anecdotal Notebook

In retrospect, we are astounded by the extreme patience of the many center directors who elected to complete our massive follow-up questionnaire. The 60 numbered items of the questionnaire (Appendix 2), in fact, amounted to well over 100 individual questions. Moreover, the first 56 items (considered in the preceding chapter) forced respondents to choose answers from lists of predetermined multiple-choice options or to fill in blanks with numbers. It was not until the last page of the questionnaire that respondents were given an opportunity to speak out in their own voices in response to three "discussion" questions (items 57 - 59).

Although we attempted to classify center directors' sometimes lengthy answers to these three questions, it was soon apparent that their statements could not be adequately summarized by classifying them and counting the various response types. Therefore, we decided to present a selection of verbatim responses to each question, allowing the providers of church-housed day care to speak directly to our readers about the problems they face and what they believe to be their strengths and successes. In selecting responses for inclusion here, we took care to represent a cross section of the opinions expressed, as identified by our initial classificatory efforts.

The Most Serious Problems Facing Providers

Center directors were asked, "What is the most serious problem you face in providing child day care?" Forty-eight percent responded in some fashion. A representative sampling of their responses is reproduced in the following pages, grouped by several dominant themes ranging from financial problems to problematic relations with host congregations. Since directors' comments often relate to more than one theme, the groupings are not mutually exclusive.

Financial Problems

The need to maintain affordable fees and still cover program costs, particularly staff salaries, propels many centers into a familiar juggling act:

- *Lexington, Massachusetts.* "We agonize over the balance between equitable salaries for staff persons (most of whom have college educations) and fees for parents. Quality day care that provides salaries that insure stability and a decent quality of life to staff is a hard juggling act. We have relatively high fees and yet staff salaries are inadequate in our minds. Who should bear this financial burden is a question we ask ourselves often."
- *Ithaca, New York.* [Our problem is] "money!! The constant struggle to make our program affordable for those who need it. The concept of serving the needy gets pushed to a back burner when the center's very existence is threatened. In the younger ages, the Board has restricted the number of subsidized children because reimbursement is well below cost. Parents have fewer and fewer affordable options; staff leave for better paying jobs."
- *Marion, Iowa.* "[Our problem is] rising costs. We have never turned down a child, and consequently have many scholarships. Now with supplies so costly, it is so difficult to keep the tuition down so that the lower-middle class can take advantage of our program. We have felt this is the 'neglected class.'"
- *Dallas, Texas.* "We find finances to be one of our biggest problems. We have not increased our tuition for the past twenty months, as the families in our care cannot afford higher fees. Yet operating costs have increased approximately 70% in the last year. Another of our most serious problems is connected to the above, [and] that is the quality of staff due to inability to pay better wages. It is very difficult to acquire staff who will further their knowledge when receiving minimum wages."
- *Fort Lauderdale, Florida.* "[My problem is] trying to keep the tuition down yet provide my staff a wage with which they can raise a family. Seventy-five percent of my staff are single-parent families."

Directors are keenly aware that in addition to their own problems in balancing budgets, rising costs will adversely affect the children and families they serve:

- *Rogers, Arkansas.* "We feel frustrated about cuts in financial assistance. We know some children are being left at home without adult supervision because their families cannot afford child care. We were totally founded to help one-income, working parents and low-income families. We find that in order to make ends meet, we must reduce salaries so we can continue to provide quality child care."

- *Beaumont, Texas*. "If there is another cut in the budget we will not be able to provide for 62 children, and 13 staff will have to be cut. Which means there will be children without anywhere to go while the parents are at work, which could lead to a high accident-rate for small children."
- *Mt. Airy, North Carolina*. [a no fee program] "The cost of providing good child care is increasing, and the members of the board would like to charge a minimum fee. Salary levels in our community are not high, and we would like to extend our services to a range of individuals. We have found working with social institutions of the state and federal level very prohibitive to the development of our program. You cannot plan a program budget with the idea of receiving state or federal funds."
- *Alexandria, Virginia*. [a parent co-op] "Rising operating costs which are forcing raises in tuition. These costs are primarily utilities and teacher salaries. We value and will not sacrifice the cornerstone of our philosophy as a cooperative, but find that rising costs are a great problem to families with only one income, which in part enables parents to 'co-op.' Parents who both work are less able to participate. In response, we have increased funds available for scholarships and accepted other persons (grandmothers, babysitters, etc.) to 'co-op.' In the face of this, we still strive for a greater racial mix and cultural diversity in our school."

High rates of unemployment exacerbate financial problems:

- *Whitehall, Ohio*. "Our biggest problem is trying to keep fees to a minimum. Our community has been badly hit by layoffs. We try to leave enough in our budget to help families in trouble."
- *Butler, Pennsylvania*. "Our bigget difficulty is keeping our head above water. We have an 18% unemployment rate in Butler County at present. People who are not working don't need day care facilities. Consequently we run in the red about six months of the year."
- *Muskegon, Michigan*. "[The problem is] high unemployment (currently 16%+)—many companies moving out of town or shutting down completely, thus fewer people can afford to pay for schooling."
- *Savanna, Illinois*. "[Our problem is] having our program survive during a time when families are losing their railroad jobs and moving away from our community. Finding and motivating low-income mothers to bring their children to preschool, and finding funding to help provide scholarships for these families."

Centers serving children with special needs may be placed under additional financial strain:

- *Cary, North Carolina.* "We integrate children with special needs into our program. One third of them have special needs, so we must keep a fairly low pupil-student ratio. Also we try to provide speech or physical therapy as needed, regardless of the parents' ability to pay for these services. Tuition does not cover the cost of these programs."

Staffing

Many directors explicitly mentioned the importance and the difficulty of finding and keeping good staff in order to maintain program quality:

- *Palo Alto, California.* "My greatest concern is the rising cost of child care, with little or no support from government. Also child care professionals are considered by society to have a very low status and to be deserving of very low salaries. We have been lucky to maintain a staff of very exceptional quality. I wonder if we will be able to continue this way."
- *Dayton, Ohio.* "The tremendous cost puts us between a rock and a hard place. Staff is terribly underpaid, but parents are not able to pay higher tuition. I have also noticed a decline in the number of qualified job applicants within the past year. Low pay and 'burnout' are forcing many child care workers in our community into other fields."
- *Miami, Florida.* "[Our problem is] finding competent bilingual staff."

Some directors, given low staffing levels, expressed fear for the safety of children:

- *Rancho Palos Verdes, California.* "When we have just one staff member left with a few children, what would we do if we had an accident?"
- *Fayetteville, North Carolina.* "I feel that we do not have enough staff to provide a completely safe environment. I realize that we are a new program—having been in operation since September 1981—and we are operating on a tight budget. I would like to know how to make this need known and understood."

Changes in the Child Care Market

Changes in local demand for child care and in preferences for particular types of programs are creating pressures for change among the providers surveyed. Some centers are affected by falling enrollment:

- *Claremont, California.* "There are so many day care facilities in this area that there are really not enough children to fill all of them. We just have one day care class that comes from 7:30 to 5:30 each day (15 children). The rest of our children are half-day and come either two, three, or five days per week. We have found that parents put their children in day care in the town in which they work, not in which they live. Claremont has no industry, so the bulk of our 15 day care children are teachers' children."

- *Urbandale, Iowa* [a parent co-op] "We have loss of enrollment due to mothers returning to the work force."
- *San Rafael, California*. "[Our problem is] declining enrollment. Our area of the country—Marin County, California—has a very high cost of living and families with young children are being forced out of the area by housing costs. Also, of those who remain here, more and more are becoming two-paycheck families. Our program, with its limited hours, does not meet the needs of families with working moms."

Other centers are faced with demand for placements that far outstrips their supply:

- *Shaker Heights, Ohio*. "We have such a need for day care in our community that it is very difficult when our sign-up time arrives. We have too many people who want to participate. We can only have twelve children per day in each class. The mothers fight for these spaces. Hard feelings sometimes result."
- *North Hollywood, California*. "Our biggest problem is lack of available space to expand to meet the needs of the 600 plus on our waiting list."
- *Fort Washington, Maryland*. "Because of the demand for child care today, the center is overwhelmed with applications for full-time care and education. The center is unable to accommodate everyone, due to limited space."

Other pressures arise from the changing needs and preferences of parents. In some communities, the demand for full-day care is growing and forcing providers to re-evaluate the services they provide:

- *Pocatello, Idaho*. "There is little need for part-time day care or preschool for children ages three to five years. Our program is designed for families with one parent in the home with the children, needing part-time care or preschool experience for their child. This type of family appears to be unique, rare, or just dwindling in numbers."
- *Pluckemin, New Jersey*. "As of now, we are a nursery school. However as more young mothers are joining the work force, I feel that a schedule more convenient to the working mother's hours should be investigated."

- *Charlotte, North Carolina.* "The challenge of moving from a morning program to providing full-day care is our most serious problem."
- *Austin, Texas.* "[Our problem is] the fact that so many parents need full-day care and we are only licensed as a half-time preschool."

Parents are also pressuring child day care providers to concern themselves more explicitly with the education of children in preparation for school:

- *Pickerington, Ohio.* "[The problem is] parents who are looking for an academic kindergarten rather than the social benefits of a preschool."
- *Cleveland, Mississippi.* "[The problem we have is] pressure to become more structured, that is, to teach the three R's."
- *Hampton, Virginia.* "Our program is a nursery program, and though we run on a daily schedule with free play, music, crafts, and play time in a separate large room with riding toys, slides, etc., some mothers expect more 'preschool' activities. Then we have to educate them as to what our program is by design and help them find another program more suited to their desires."
- *Austin, Texas.* "[Our problem is] facing the constant pressure to push kids faster and faster into formal sit-down reading and writing activities."

Among directors responding to the follow-up questionnaire, a few reported that they were unable to adapt to changes in the marketplace and would have to close their doors:

- *Peoria, Illinois.* "We are closing our doors September 1, 1982, because of inadequate registration—only four children. We are licensed for 16. The unemployment in Peoria has forced many out of work, and we are competing with in-home day care. Sadly, we are closing after 12 years. We were the first licensed infant day care center in Peoria."

Parent Relations/Support

Parents of children figure importantly in the concerns of center directors. Center staff sometimes find it difficult to communicate effectively with parents and to reconcile different views and values:

- *Inverness, Florida.* "The most serious problem we face is parental relations. Conflicting views and values have made the cooperative nature of our school a continuous challenge."
- *Cocoa Beach, Florida.* "We do not provide day care services, only preschool. Our greatest problem is educating parents as to the

needs of children. Parents appear to want children to learn formal skills early."

- *Aurora, Missouri.* "[The problem we face is] communicating with parents honestly and openly when their child lacks average skills or intelligence or maturity."
- *Gaithersburg, Maryland.* "[Our problem is] communicating honestly, but tactfully, with parents."

Difficulties in dealing with parents are heightened when actual or potential child abuse/neglect is present:

- *Brighton, Michigan.* "The program has been in effect for three years. The past year revealed serious problems of both physical and emotional child abuse. We have begun to deal with the problem in a constructive manner: both individual as well as group discussions and support are employed."
- *Evansville, Indiana.* "Our most serious problem is gaining the trust of potential child abusers. We want them to use our nursery in times of stress without feeling that they will be labeled as child abusers."
- *Traverse City, Michigan.* "Our day care program is for children who have been victimized by domestic violence in whatever form it may take. The biggest problem we face is educating people to the fact that it does exist beyond a few isolated cases, and thereby convincing people that there is a need for such a program. Domestic violence is ugly. Perhaps that is one of the reasons why people choose to ignore the facts. Ignorance in this case is certainly not bliss but disaster."

The growing number of single-parent families in America poses additional challenges for child day care providers. Some explicitly recognized the special needs of these families:

- *Covina, California.* "I wish our center were able to do more for the single parent. We have approximately thirty single-parent families in our center, each struggling in their way to keep afloat."

Relation of Center to Community

A number of respondents reflected on the sometimes uncertain place of child day care programs in their communities:

- *Fayetteville, North Carolina.* "...we try to make the complexion of the preschool program mesh with the community in which it is located—the inner city. This is an elitist organization in the midst of a rugged section, and our tendency is to create an oasis. ...We could serve more special children if the agencies in our area would do more referrals. Being in a military town, we never know how many children we will have. Families move in and out very often."

- *Oneida, New York.* "[We face] the problem of community acceptance and support—day care is not an accepted priority. There is considerable resistance from the county Social Services Department, from political leaders and other community organizations. We are the only licensed day care center in the county. One child in the county is receiving county assistance at present. All services for children, including child welfare, protection, and prevention, are minimal."
- *Niagara Falls, New York.* "Niagara Falls is made up of several strong ethnic groups. People in the older generation are opposed to day care for their grandchildren. Day care needs a more positive image. A series of articles in the Buffalo Evening News recently was especially harmful."

Lack of Knowledge/Methods

The comments reproduced here reflect an awareness of needs for staff training and support and sometimes express explicit needs for personal or programmatic guidance:

- *Greensboro, North Carolina.* "[Our problem is] training staff to deal with children who are presenting discipline problems."
- *Milwaukee, Wisconsin.* "[The problem is] realizing that for many of these children you are their parental figure. Making sure that we each make the right decisions and don't become too emotionally involved."
- *Kilgore, Texas.* "[Our problem is] keeping the teachers alert and interested in all types of children's learning experiences, and encouraging them to attempt them."
- *Fairview, Kansas.* "I hope you will be able to help me. Our program has grown so that I need management skills I don't have."
- *Altoona, Pennsylvania.* "Our teachers are good, but our program could be better if we had some sort of curriculum for four- and five-year-olds."

Directors of programs that include religious education were especially expressive of the need for program materials. Most commonly they acknowledged the inadequacy of Sunday school materials for daily preschools. A half dozen respondents reported that, failing to find adequate curricular materials, they have developed their own.

Relation with Congregation/Church

Of special concern to us were instances in which center directors reported difficulties in their relations with host congregations. Their comments raise a range of issues:

- *Malvern, Pennsylvania.* "Two problems of equal importance that face the center are the relationship between the church and the center and the lack of expansion space. Current pastoral support of the center is very positive. However, the lay leadership is generally quite unsupportive, and at times the relationship seems to be one of adversaries rather than cooperating agencies, even though officially the center is labeled by the church as a community outreach project."
- *Fort Lauderdale, Florida.* "We also have a problem with the older people in the host church. They don't want their church filled with little black children dirtying their church walls and using their Sunday school rooms."
- *Knoxville, Tennessee.* "Aside from constantly trying to maintain a balanced budget we face problems within the church congregation. It seems our church is equally divided, half hate day care and half are very supportive."
- *Adel, Iowa.* "...in our church there is a group very supportive of day care and a very unsupportive group and a number of people who don't know much about day care in the church. The unsupportive group does not attack the *quality* of our program; rather, their objection is to any group using the building, except on Sundays and then by members only. They do not want the church to be part of the community; they seek to keep it for themselves. Our most serious problem is whether the church will continue to house day care at all."
- *Lockhart, Texas.* "The local church is fearful that the school may cost the church money and is still waiting to see the school fail, although it is in its fifth year."
- *Norwood, Ohio.* "The problems are related to the church: (1) limited space, with no room for expansion, (2) pressure to keep children quiet during church meetings, (3) rooms unavailable because of meetings, (4) responsibility for cleaning rooms that other groups have used, (5) locking up and putting away equipment so that it won't be broken, and (6) non-acceptance of handicapped children."

Concluding Note

We were struck again and again by the insight and wisdom of comments offered us. Clearly the providers of church-housed child care have much to contribute to continuing efforts to analyze child care needs and problems and to formulate possible solutions.

The Greatest Strengths/Successes of Programs

The second open-ended question posed to center directors asked, "What is the greatest strength of your program? What are you doing most effectively?" Sixty-eight percent of directors responded. The most frequently mentioned strength/success were providing "quality care." Next most frequent was meeting the special needs of children and families. The comments quoted below are organized by major themes.

Quality Care

Center directors frequently mentioned able and caring staff as a vital ingredient in program quality:

- *St. Mary's Ohio.* "[Our greatest strength is] care given to the children by a concerned staff. The educational aspect of the program we offer, which is in cooperation with our local school system."
- *Havelock, North Carolina.* "The strength of our program is in the caring staff. Our children feel quite comfortable in bringing any of their problems to any member of the staff."
- *Fayetteville, North Carolina.* "I feel that since we are a small group with a congenial staff, we are able to provide more individual attention and to gear any instruction given to meet the needs of different children."

Often, too, the high quality of care was attributed to the overall tone or atmosphere of the center:

- *Columbia, South Carolina.* "We are providing a learning environment that is bright, open, and varied enough to challenge all of the child's senses. We truly have children who enjoy coming to school, and because of this we have very few discipline problems."
- *Dallas, Texas.* "[We have] the desire to provide quality day care for

children of all economic standings, not just the extremely poor, or the wealthy, but children of lower-middle income who cannot get subsidies. [We have] faith in God and man to help provide the means of accomplishing these goals."

- *Jasper, Indiana*. "We are open to all children, and have raised standards of preschool in the city. We are the first church to sponsor and operate a preschool. We give children well-rounded learning experiences without emphasizing academics like numbers and the alphabet. We create an atmosphere of caring and respect for individual children."
- *Cleveland, Ohio*. "Staff, parents, children, and church members care about one another, like one another, and are mutually supportive. This creates a warm, nurturing environment for the children."

Positive Child Outcomes

Many directors explicitly linked success in providing quality care with positive outcomes for children:

- *Newark, Delaware*. "[We try] to guide the children toward further training with an early start in education in mind. We aim to guide teaching activities toward the development of skills and work habits to be used in the future. We stress spiritual development of children to attempt to guide standards and attitudes, but we do not stress any one faith or religion."
- *Minneapolis, Minnesota*. "[We are] helping children form a positive self-image."
- *Bartlesville, Oklahoma*. "We are giving children a chance to learn social and learning skills in a caring Christian atmosphere. Our program is low-key, so children can discover that learning is fun."
- *Grand Rapids, Michigan*. "[We are] helping children to grow and build their own self-concepts."
- *Gaithersburg, Maryland*. "[We are] training the children to work with groups and to give and take successfully."

Service to Mothers

Some directors perceived their programs' greatest contribution as a service to mothers:

- *Reedsport, Oregon*. "[We are] freeing women in our community to address needs in their lives."
- *Burbank, California*. "[We are] filling needs of mothers with young children in this community for time to themselves. Also, filling needs of children for playtime with other children, as our

community has a rapidly dwindling population of young children due to unaffordable housing."

Ministry

Directors of programs incorporating religious education components sometimes viewed the strengths of their programs in light of the larger evangelical and social ministry of their churches:

- *Ellenton, Florida.* "[We are] reaching families in our area who normally wouldn't attend church."
- *Moscow, Idaho.* "[Our program] provides outreach to the church, and introduces the church and pastor to the preschoolers and their parents."
- *Shinnston, West Virginia.* "Our greatest strength comes from our faith in God! And the power of prayer."
- *Whitehall, Ohio.* "Our program has encouraged many unchurched families to join our worship and send their children to our Sunday and summer Bible schools."

Unique Features of Program

Among the most interesting of responses were those describing strengths in terms of the program's responsiveness to particular local circumstances:

- *Whiteville, North Carolina.* "[We are] offering quality child care to all age groups in a rural environment where this has never been a concern, making the community aware of the specific needs of infants, toddlers, preschool-age children."
- *El Sobrante, California.* "We do not provide child day care. We operate a parent participation nursery school sponsored through the school district. Parents attend classes, work in the participation program, provide transportation, maintain grounds and equipment, pay monthly fees of $30, organize play groups and car pools. It is an extremely well-run program and has been operating for over 30 years!"
- *Poteet, Texas.* "The pastor is very interested in this program. There is a great need for day care in this area, but mothers must bring the children to town for the program, as half of our population is rural, and this may be a deterrent. We have four rooms immediately available and could expand if enrollment grows."
- *Schenectady, New York.* "The program itself—we have a 'family' program. We accept all preschool children within a family for a single fee. The fee is the same for each family regardless of the

number of children. The families are very supportive of one another."

- *Fort Lauderdale, Florida*. "We were started 14 years ago with the idea to help low-income families. There are not many places that can help these families. We offer a strong preschool program with day care on each end. For many of our children, we are the only stable thing in their lives, and the food they get from us is all they may get. The strong hands-on preschool program may make the difference of the children being held over in public kindergarten or passing on to first grade. ...I think the major thing that holds the whole program together is that we love our jobs and love the children and feel that what we are doing is acting out our Christian belief."

Concluding Note

Visits by Child Day Care Project staff to numerous centers across the country have only reinforced the impression that these comments leave: provision of quality care is *the* major concern of local child care providers. While there seems to be growing agreement about certain basic or minimal conditions for program quality—staff training, staff/child ratio, group size, physical environment—there remains considerable diversity of opinion among both parents and providers about the full meaning of quality child care. As long as we remain a society of diverse cultural and religious traditions, it is inevitable that we should disagree among ourselves about the meanings of "quality" in different spheres of life. Our different notions of quality child care and the variety of child care actually offered bespeak this pluralism.

The Impacts of State and Federal Budget Cuts

In the spring of 1982 as we prepared to mail the second questionnaire, a round of anticipated federal budget cuts to social service programs was announced. This announcement followed close on the heels of a first round of cuts made in January 1982. We wanted to gain at least some insight into the effects of these cuts on local programs. To that end we asked, "Do you expect federal and state budget cuts to affect your program? If so, describe the impact of these cuts and how you plan to respond to them." Only 28% of center directors responded. Of that number, 6% said they were not sure how they would be affected. The remainder detailed for us the consequences they foresaw.

General Economic Downturn

A number of respondents felt that they would not be directly influenced by budget cuts (presumably because they do not receive public monies) but described the consequence of the general economic downturn and inflation, which in part had inspired the budget cuts:

- *Norwalk, Iowa.* "More mothers will go to work and they still want day care, not preschool. Also preschool is a luxury, not a necessity. Parents who must economize will cut out our program."
- *Massapequa, New York.* "Out-of-work parents become scholarship families, putting a strain on our budget. Also the part-week child is on an upswing. Parents are becoming two-job families. We do not, as a rule, serve parents who both work because we provide only half-day sessions."

Even in a suburban community near Washington, D.C., a director worried about the administrative outcome for her program:

- *College Park, Maryland.* "Yes, if these families start losing their jobs because of cutbacks...to put government workers on furlough. These parents won't be able to continue to send their children. A lot come to our program because they want their children to have a preschool experience but cannot afford expensive preschools."

Others wondered what new political challenges and bureaucratic complexities would be ushered in by the budget cuts:

- *Paris, Kentucky.* "[We will be affected] not in money per se, but in the increased data gathering and paper work that will follow. However, every year we are anxious as the federal dollars are allocated and then as Kentucky deals with the allocations. Political forces affect the use of this money."

Child Care Food Program

More respondents (30%) mentioned cuts in the Child Care Food Program than in any other single program:

- *Montgomery, Alabama.* "We anticipate perhaps losing the reimbursement we receive from the Child Care Food Program. We feel we would have to alter our menu content somewhat, reducing quality, quantity, and diversity."
- *Phoenix, Arizona.* "Cuts in the Child Care Food Program may have an impact. Because our children receive most of their food at the center, we offer two hot meals and an afternoon supplement. We have always allowed our children to eat all they desire. This cutback may result in our having to limit food to some extent; however, the minimum daily requirements will always be offered."

- *San Francisco, California.* "Yes, Food Program was cut by one third. We are substituting cheaper cuts of meat and just *barely* meeting minimum requirements. We need to raise $3,000 next year to keep the program going."
- *Oneida, New York.* "USDA food reimbursement reductions and CETA—teacher aide, maintenance, salary losses—have had a great impact on us. We are at present losing $2,000 a month. We plan additional fund raising and cooperative programs with the ARC (Association for Retarded Children) as well as a wraparound kindergarten program to expand our program and increase our income source."
- *Tulsa, Oklahoma.* "We lost over $13,000 in school lunch money and commodities in 1982. We anticipate further cuts in 1983. Fund raising has become a major aspect of our program."
- *Dallas, Texas.* "Yes, I am sure if the programs are cut deeply enough, we will be affected. However, we are thinking ahead for such an eventuality. Our [church women's group] are harvesting vegetables from our garden spot project, which we hope to carry over into next year."
- *Greenville, South Carolina.* "Only cuts in lunch and nutrition programs will affect our program. Fees will have to be increased and nutrition may be hurt."
- *Lima, Ohio.* "If the food program is cut and/or minimum wage is increased, we will have to raise rates."
- *Racine, Wisconsin.* "We benefited from a state milk program in 1982 that provided milk for our children at a very low cost. This program may be cut for the 1982-83 school year, which means we must provide a beverage of lower quality nutritionally, and at our cost."
- *Cleveland, Ohio.* "The food program cuts have been drastic, and we need the help from that program. We were cut to a fourth of what we were getting. Our reponse at one point was to raise tuition, but we do not feel we can do that again at this point. Many parents' incomes have been cut."

Not all directors oppose the budget cuts, however:

- *Las Vegas, Nevada.* "The cuts in food programs will affect us. We will raise our rates slightly to offset this. I believe the cuts are justified."

Eligibility Changes

Changes in the eligibility of poor children and families for public subsidies was another area of concern:

- *Kittanning, Pennsylvania.* "We used to have an enrollment of 140-150 children and a budget of $412,000. We are down to 95 children and a budget of $225,000. Staff has gone from 50 to 24, plus CETA workers. I expect...even further cuts. Obviously we have laid off staff. Present staff does all janitorial work. No equipment is being bought. Some staff are doing two jobs. We use more volunteers."
- *Colby, Kansas.* "We used to have over 30 children receiving financial assistance from the state; we now have seven because there is not money to help more of them. This does not really hurt the center because we can reduce staff, but I don't know what all those people who need help with paying for day care are doing."
- *Dayton, Ohio.* "Due to Title XX and Title IV cuts, we are being asked to enroll children who have been dropped from eligibility. We are attempting to provide care for these children, but only for a few of them. Other children are dropping out of our program due to parents' job cutbacks or layoffs."
- *Yellow Springs, Ohio.* "Title XX cuts will mean fewer children in our programs. We have to raise the bottom of our sliding fee scale, necessitating an increasing burden on our lower-middle-income families."
- *Ithaca, New York.* "Regarding Title XX and AFDC: Fewer parents are eligible, but they still cannot afford our fee scale. We are raising funds to create a scholarship fund, but this will only cover a small number of families."
- *Poughkeepsie, New York.* "We expect cutbacks in federal and state funding. They will have a drastic effect on the center. We will be forced to eliminate some classrooms which are more expensive to operate, namely, Infants and Toddlers. Ironically, this is the area which is most needed in the community."
- *Ames, Iowa.* "The recent cuts have already severely affected all our programs. In Title XX funds alone, our agency's income has dropped from $140,000 to a projected $3,000. The most severe impact has been the growing inaccessibility of our services to low-income families. There are no longer sufficient Title XX funds for low-income families, and as an agency, we cannot afford to subsidize these families, either. Families must therefore make less expensive, often inadequate, child care arrangements."
- *Worchester, Massachusetts.* "Since we are committed by mission to the low-income consumer, these cuts could force severe changes in the program or even the closing of the center. There is no evidence of enough private funds to make up for the loss of these public monies."

Cutbacks in Other Governmental Programs

Programs serving specialized populations also experienced difficulty as a result of budget cuts:

- *Buffalo, New York.* "Yes, enrollment of state and county children has dropped by almost 75%, which has dropped the total enrollment from 48 children to 25. We are not sure if we can respond to something like this other than to encourage these clients to fight the legislature that determines the budget."
- *Erlanger, Kentucky.* "Recent cuts have already affected our day care by forcing a handicapped child to drop out because of lack of funding."
- *Port Angeles, Washington.* "Yes, we had to cut individual speech and physical therapies. We provide evaluations and supervision of our program by these specialists. We are having people use private insurance, SSI, or Crippled Children's Service to provide these. Also, we are cutting back the number of days that a child attends from a maximum of four to three days a week."
- *South Bend, Indiana.* [a Head Start center] "While the Head Start appropriation has not suffered cuts , the agencies to which families are referred have been drastically cut, which does affect them."
- *Appleton, Wisconsin.* "Recent federal and state cuts have limited the amount of center care available to low-income families. In 1982, [our program] is operating without a $70,000 contract to offer language development to Hmong refugees' children. We raised $30,000 in private money for scholarships and have cut back the number of children served. AFDC and low-income parents are encouraged to use private, certified babysitters because it is cheaper for the county, so center enrollment drops."

Unspecified Cuts

Several directors told us of the difficulties encountered by their programs, without stipulating which particular program cuts were causing the difficulty:

- *Athens, Ohio.* "Our budget has been cut to subsistence level—salaries, rent, utilities. We can only cut staff further, which would mean serving fewer children."
- *Minneapolis, Minnesota.* "We have lost one third of our enrollment because of cuts, lost jobs, reduced welfare funds, and so on. We hope by advertising to attract parents who are still employed."
- *Manitowoc, Wisconsin.* "Have already been cut! We now charge for our classes; it was a free program."
- *Minneapolis, Minnesota.* "Yes, when the government makes cuts,

first, it affects our enrollment, and second, it causes the fees to rise to cover our expenses."

- *La Porte City, Iowa*. "Without state aid, our program will not benefit from teacher education (the only "fringe" our teachers receive) or be able to purchase quality equipment."

Fighting the Cuts

Many directors reported their own or coalitional efforts to make legislators aware of the consequences of the budget cuts and to seek reinstatement of previous eligibility criteria and funding levels:

- *San Francisco, California*. "Recent federal and state cuts have knocked out $40,000 of our $200,000 budget. This has had drastic effects on us. We have to cut back staff hours and we are afraid the quality of our program will decline. We have lobbied hard with our legislators to little avail."
- *Tacoma, Washington*. "Some cuts are already affecting us through government fees for licensing. We have petitioned the bill and will be seeking a waiver of fees."
- *Albuquerque, New Mexico*. "We are currently dealing with these cutbacks. The method for addressing these involved educating New Mexico and U.S. legislators about early intervention. Staff and parents waiting for services are encouraged to write their legislators, and while the New Mexico legislative session is in progress, parents and staff attend pertinent sessions. Lobbying occurs year round."
- *Seattle, Washington*. "State budget cuts have already affected our program. We are affiliated with our local community college. In the past, they were able to provide us with a staff member to conduct our parent education program. This past year, the budget cuts to the college eliminated our parent instructor. We have an active group representing us at our state legislature and have all participated in a massive letter writing campaign to our legislators."

Giving Up

Yet, for some the difficulties seemed overwhelming. Despite plans to lobby for greater government support, some respondents felt they would not be able to await a better day:

- *Big Rapids, Michigan*. "Yes, it will eventually effect the closing of many centers, those whose main resources were from government support."

- *Shenandoah, Iowa.* "Yes, they already have. Our government money, mainly through the Child Care Food Program, was cut 70%, which has hurt us a great deal—to the extent that when our savings are spent, we will have to close our doors."
- *Marion, Kansas.* "No, we are no longer in operation...due to lack of community financial support."

Concluding Note

These responses remind us again of the precarious state of local child care finances and the vulnerability of programs, children, and families—especially those from lower-income groups. We could scarcely read providers' comments without renewing our own commitment to work toward the formation of an extended dialogue about child care policy. It is here most profoundly that the Church must find its voice.

V
Epilogue

Once to every man and nation
Comes the moment to decide,
In the strife of truth with falsehood,
For the good or evil side.

New occasions teach new duties,
Time makes ancient good uncouth;
They must upward still and onward,
Who would keep abreast of truth.
James Russell Lowell (1819-1891)

We began the book with a line from this familiar hymn, which both warns and instructs believers that "new occasions teach new duties." The Child Day Care Project has revealed many new occasions. The dissolution of old myths and the acquisition of new information about child care in local parishes challenge the Church, through the ecumenical organization of the National Council of Churches (NCC), to once again learn new duties. Never in Christian history have new duties been quickly and universally agreed upon, and we have no reason to believe this occasion will be an exception. Through its unique and often curious process of discernment, the Church must find its vocation and role in relation to child care. It is not for us to define that role. Rather, as members of the community for whom "the moment to decide" has come, it is for us to state as clearly as we are able the truths that prescribe our new occasion.

We hope that the remaining pages of this book will serve as a bridge between research and action. First, we summarize responses to the last question of the follow-up survey: "Would you like to be part of a network of church day care providers?" These responses suggest specific directions in which the Church might move. Next, we share the conclusions we have reached from our experiences in the Child Day Care Project. Last, we outline a set of issues and recommend general directions that might focus and guide deliberations about possible roles for the Church in relation to child day care. For those outside the Church but within the child care world, we hope that our observations and suggestions will be signs that the Church is moving, however ponderously, toward a more self-conscious role.

Seeking Community

The final item of our lengthy follow-up questionnaire asked, "Would you like to be part of a network of church day care providers?" Forty percent answered "yes"; 17%, "no"; and 43%, "not sure."

Many persons who answered "no" and "not sure" also wrote marginal notes explaining their responses; about 100 others were contacted by telephone to determine the reasons for their uncertainty or lack of interest. We learned that many directors of church-housed programs wanted more information before deciding whether they were interested: Would the proposed network concern itself with religious education? Would it offer services useful to their types of programs? Would directors of independently operated programs be allowed to join? And so on. A major source of confusion and doubt among providers was our wording of the question. By saying, "a network of *church* day care providers," we put off a number of persons who operate independent, secular, child day care programs. We meant to say, "a network of *church-housed* day care providers." Finally, in spite of definitions to the contrary, our use of the term "day care" in the title of the project and throughout the questionnaire was unfortunately interpreted by some directors as excluding their "nursery school," "preschool," "playgroup," or other program not offering full-day care.

Of respondents who indicated that they would like to participate in a network of providers, we further asked, "...what would you like the network to do?" Six possible areas of work were listed, and respondents were asked to suggest any other ideas they might have. Providers indicated that the most important thing a network could do would be to "share information on program resources"; 90% of respondents checked this item. Next most popular were "provide staff training resources" (selected by 71%) and "raise consciousness of church regarding church-related child day care" (selected by 70%). Despite great concerns about financial difficulties expressed in response to an earlier question, only 57% indicated that they would like a network of providers to "share fund-raising ideas." Fifty-one percent selected "provide legislative information"; 46%, "coordinate advocacy efforts." Eight percent of respondents had other suggestions, including help in securing health insurance, life insurance, and pension benefits at group rates; developing strategies for covering start-up costs; and organizing national meetings.

Face-to-face meetings with church-housed providers during visits to individual centers across the country and at a series of small, regional conferences have revealed more interest in network building and participation than was indicated by the follow-up survey. In general, any initial reservations about participation are quickly replaced by enthusiasm as common interests are discovered and a network's potential for addressing critical needs is explored and appreciated. Usually providers recognize, as we have, that the Church offers an infrastructure through which providers can be identified and contacted. All that we have learned of their aspirations for a church-related network of child care providers points up the importance of the Church's further consideration of its role in child care.

The 15 denominations or communions that participated in the study are now confronted with an embarassment of riches. They possess new and more complete information about their roles in child care. They are in contact with nearly 10,000 providers who have begun to develop a voice and who are expressing needs for coordination and support. At this new occasion, national agencies of the Church, individually and collectively, must ask new questions about their own continuing role in child care.

Our Conclusions

The major conclusions we have drawn from this study and from the larger work of the Child Day Care Project serve as working assumptions for the continuing efforts of the NCC's Child Advocacy Office on behalf of children and their families. We share these conclusions/assumptions, knowing that they are incomplete and imperfect, but hoping that they will provide grist for further conversations within the Church and between Church agencies and child care advocates.

The Church is a major provider of child care in this nation. As such, it is a major factor—however unintentional—in any national debate about child care. Time has brought us to a point where the "ancient good" may be "uncouth." Our evidence suggests that child care in the churches requires more intentionality on the part of national church agencies if the quantity and quality of care offered is to continue and increase. The time has come for both the Church and the child care community to recognize the Church's very significant role in child care and to act in light of this knowledge.

Church-housed child care has remarkable strengths. Many of these strengths have been stated or implied throughout the text of this report:

- A diversity of program types serving a multiplicity of needs
- A broad base of funding and in-kind support that makes it economically more robust than child care provisions in general

- Grassroots sensitivity to changing family needs for child care services
- Adaptability and flexibility in meeting these changing needs
- Experienced and able staff
- Generally sufficient structure and organization to provide reliable and stable community-based child care

Any initiative the Church might take with respect to child care in local parishes should recognize and build upon these strengths.

Church-housed child care providers face numerous problems and challenges. Many of these difficulties are common to child care nationally; some are peculiar to church-housed programs. All result in a variety of needs that national church agencies should assume will persist:

- Low levels of status and acceptance of providers—generally, as is common among other child care providers; particularly, in relation to church congregations
- Vulnerability to fluctuations in the child care market and to changes in public policy and funding, producing financial planning and management difficulties
- Considerable staff instability and turnover, which suggests a need for job enrichment to include increased wages and benefits; continuing education and job advancement potential; and for directors, opportunities to acquire increased financial and personal management skills
- A dearth of quality curriculum and program resource materials at affordable cost and an acute need for religiously oriented curricular materials designed for day care programs that include a religious education dimension
- A sense of isolation from professional colleagues and issues and a need for low cost mechanisms to enable church-housed providers to be in contact with each other and with other child care providers, church agencies, and child advocacy organizations
- A frequently expressed need for a variety of technical assistance services related to needs assessment, start-up financing, general management, and so forth
- In some instances, a need for incentives and capacity to improve the quality of care provided.

Any effort to address such needs and problems should certainly include careful consideration of the impacts particular actions might have on existing strengths of church-housed child care.

Issues and Directions

The National Council of Churches and its member communions undertook this study in order to obtain the information necessary for developing an informed advocacy stance regarding child day care. The precise form their future initiatives will take, the order in which they will be undertaken, and the extent to which they will be undertaken by or in conjunction with non-church agencies are decisions properly left to church agencies and providers. Nonetheless, in these deliberations, we believe that the following issues and possible directions for action should be weighed.

Development of a Statement of Policy and Purpose

The development of a comprehensive statement of policy and purpose, endorsed by national church agencies, would provide a valuable opportunity for the churches to clarify their thinking about child care programming. Such a statement would also help others, both in the child care community and in governmental agencies, understand more clearly the perspective of the Church—or at least of that segment represented by the NCC—on child care. Recent regional conferences sponsored by the Child Advocacy Working Group of the National Council of Churches have demonstrated great need for and interest in such a statement among church-housed providers, local church agencies, and others.

Network Development

The methods employed by the Child Day Care Project to study church-housed child care produced a mailing list containing the names and addresses of some 10,000 directors of church-housed child day care centers. Currently, most of these providers are not in contact with any national early childhood or child care organization. Interest on the part of providers in an ecumenical child care network was suggested by the follow-up survey and confirmed through regional conferences of providers. A network of providers might take many forms and could be expanded to include denominations not participating in the original study. Such a network would relieve the isolation felt by many providers and stimulate an exchange of ideas, which would be valuable not only to church-housed programs but also to secular child-advocates, policy makers, and national church agencies.

Coalition

In clarifying its own goals and policy perspectives, the Church will wish to enter into conversations and, when mutually beneficial, into coalitions with a wide range of national organizations involved with various aspects of child advocacy and early childhood care and education. Existing as they do in a nation lacking comprehensive child care policies, U.S. churches may gain much and contribute substantially to the national dialogue about child care.

Further Study

The work of the Child Day Care Project provides an initial mapping of church-housed child care but fails to answer a number of important questions and has raised many others. The ecumenical community might build upon the present work by designing and conducting selected programs of further study. Such programs might take up any number of issues identified in this book and/or address issues that lie outside the domain of church-housed child care considered here. More knowledge is needed if sound policies are to be developed, and the Church is in a unique position to acquire this knowledge by virtue of its access to a major portion of the child day care services offered in this country.

Provision of Technical Assistance

It is vividly apparent that local parishes and church-housed child care providers need a broad range of technical assistance. Local providers and congregations are quick to detail their needs for support, and the ecumenical community will need to sort through these diverse requests to determine which can be served by existing non-church agencies, which might be served best at local or regional levels, and which require the resources of national church agencies. Considerations of effectiveness, cost, and policy compatibility must figure centrally in these deliberations.

Specific Needs for Program Resources

The need for program resource materials might have been considered under "technical assistance" but was mentioned so frequently that we have treated it separately here. Church-housed child care providers very much want help in learning about available program resource materials and in choosing among them. The costs of such materials are often prohibitive to small programs and to those on especially tight budgets. Church agencies might explore ways to help church-housed providers gain access to much-needed program materials, while still providing for a variety of program approaches responsive to varying local needs and preferences.

Of particular interest to the churches should be the needs that some providers expressed for religious education materials appropriate for young children. Who better than national church agencies to develop such materials?

A Concluding Note

Our observations lead us to believe that church-housed child care, in its current form, is generally robust and full-functioning, but that the strengths born of its entrepreneurial and grassroots nature must be carefully guarded from the potentially negative effects of over-enthusiastic institutionalization, however well meaning. Having said this, we also believe that certain initiatives can be taken with some confidence that they will do more good than harm. Thus, we strongly recommend that the churches participating in the NCC Child Advocacy Working Group chart a course of action along the lines just suggested.

In addition to the six general issues we have already outlined, there will from time to time be specific issues of urgent concern to which national church agencies will want to respond. An example of such an issue is the current inclination of state governments to exempt churches from child care and education licensing requirements. As is apparent from our study, most programs housed in churches are licensed. Our direct contacts with church-housed providers, including directors of church-operated programs, have revealed their unanimous insistence that programs located in churches be held accountable for meeting licensing requirements. The National Council of Churches will likely wish to use its considerable resources to express its point of view on this matter. In order to speak to this and other urgent issues in a thoughtful and effective voice, national church agencies will want to draw on the knowledge and experience of providers within their own network and of secular child-advocates.

The authors are acutely aware that theirs has been a rare privilege—the opportunity to share with thousands of centers and perhaps millions of families the concern for child care. The hymn to which we have so often referred concludes:

They must upward still and onward,
Who would keep abreast of truth.

Keeping abreast of truth in child care will require intelligence, insight, and sensitivity. Our hope is that the Church and the child care community will together resolve to find these abilities.

A child care provider working in one of the churches surveyed will have the last word, for her simple summary is eloquent in its wisdom and accuracy. From a small Texas town she writes:

> "May God bless you in your work. Our center serves children from low-income and middle-class families. Their parents are working as hard as they can. But society has to care, the Church, the government, directors and teachers, all of us. It is the only way..."

Appendix 1
Initial Questionnaire

Nº 3415

CHILD DAY CARE QUESTIONNAIRE

1. Does your congregation operate or house any child day care program? 1___yes 2___no (Go to Question #3) (8)

2. If "YES," please provide us with the following information about each program that is operated by or housed in your congregation.

TYPES OF PROGRAMS IN YOUR CONGREGATION (Check all that apply)	RELATIONSHIP TO CONGREGATION (Check one response) Operated by congregation	Rental/Use Agreement	IS PROGRAM LIMITED TO FAMILIES OF YOUR CONGREGATION (Check yes or no)		NAME OF PROGRAM DIRECTOR(S) (Please PRINT)
(9)___infant day care	(17) 1___	2___	(25) 1___yes	2___no	___
___toddler day care	1___	2___	1___yes	2___no	___
___day care for disabled children	1___	2___	1___yes	2___no	___
___pre-school educational program	1___	2___	1___yes	2___no	___
___after school program - daily	1___	2___	1___yes	2___no	___
___emergency drop-off care	1___	2___	1___yes	2___no	___
___mother's program	1___	2___	1___yes	2___no	___
(16)___other___ (please specify)	(24) 1___	2___	(32) 1___yes	2___no	___

3. Which of the following best describes the community in which your congregation is located? (33)

1___central core of a major metropolitan area

2___fringe of a major metropolitan area: densely populated - e.g., apartments, small lots

3___fringe of a major metropolitan area: suburban, e.g., large lots, open spaces

4___small city or town

5___rural farming community

6___rural non-farming community

4. With which of the following denominations is your congregation affiliated? (Check all that apply.) (34-43)

01___African Methodist Episcopal

02___African Methodist Episcopal Zion Church

03___American Baptist Churches in the U.S.A.

04___American Lutheran Church

05___Christian Church (Disciples of Christ)

06___Christian Methodist Episcopal Church

07___The Episcopal Church

08___Greek Orthodox Archdiocese of North and South America

09___Lutheran Church in America

10___The Presbyterian Church in the United States

11___Progressive National Baptist Convention, Inc.

12___Reformed Church in America

13___United Church of Christ

14___The United Methodist Church

15___The United Presbyterian Church in the U.S.A.

16___other___ (please specify)

Church Name and Mailing Address: ___ (name)

PLEASE PRINT: ___ (street address)

___ (city) (state) (zip)

Appendix 2
Follow-up Questionnaire

Col.s (1-8)
CD #'1' = (9)

NATIONAL COUNCIL OF CHURCHES OF CHRIST, U.S.A.

CHILD DAY CARE PROJECT

QUESTIONNAIRE FOR CHILD CARE PROGRAMS OPERATED ON CHURCH PREMISES

Name of Program ______________________________

Name of Director ______________________________

Name of church in which program is located:

____

Address(including zip code) ______________________________

____

____

Telephone number (   ) ______________________________

SECTION I: BASIC PROGRAM INFORMATION

The following questions (1-24) will enable us to understand the type(s) of program(s) that you operate, their hours of operation, etc. IF YOU OPERATE ANY OF THE FOLLOWING PROGRAMS FOR 3-5 YEAR OLDS - NURSERY SCHOOL, HEADSTART, DAY CARE, MONTESSORI, PLAYGROUPS (NOT KINDERGARTEN) - PLEASE ANSWER THE QUESTIONS UNDER COLUMN C FOR PRE-SCHOOL.

1. Do you provide weekday programs to any of the following age groups?

INFANTS (age birth to 2 years)	TODDLERS (age 18 months to 3 years)	PRE-SCHOOLERS (age 3 to 5 years)
(10)1___NO	1___NO (29)	1___NO (48)
2___YES If Yes, please answer all questions in COLUMN A	2___YES If Yes, please answer all questions in COLUMN B	2___YES If Yes, please answer all questions in COLUMN C
COLUMN A	COLUMN B	COLUMN C
2. At what hour does your infant program open? ___:___ (11-13) At what hour does it close? ___:___ (14-16)	At what hour does your toddler program open? ___:___ (30-32) At what hour does it close? ___:___ (33-35)	At what hour does your pre-school program open? ___:___ (49-51) At what hour does it close? ___:___ (52-54)
3. How many days per week does this program operate? (17)Circle One: 1 2 3 4 5 6 7	How many days per week does this program operate? Circle One: 1 2 3 4 5 6 7 (36)	How many days per week does this program operate Circle ONE: 1 2 3 4 5 6 7 (55)
4. How many months of the year does program operate? ______number (18-19)	How many months of the year does program operate? ______number (37-38)	How many months of the year does program operate? ______number (56-57)
5. How many groups/classrooms do you operate for infants? ______number (20-21)	How many groups/classrooms do you operate for toddlers? ______number (39-40)	How many groups/classrooms do you operate for pre-schoolers? ______number (58-59)
6. What is the current enrollment in this program? ______number (22-24)	What is the current enrollment in this program? ______number (41-43)	What is the current enrollment in this program? ______number (60-62)
7. What is the maximum number of infants you can enroll in this program? ______number (25-27)	What is the maximum number of toddlers you can enroll in this program? ______number (44-46)	What is the maximum number of pre-schoolers you can enroll in this program? ______number (63-65)
8. At 11:00 a.m., what is the approximate staff*/child ratio in this program? (Check number that is closest to your situation.)	At 11:00 a.m., what is the approximate staff*/child ratio in this program? (Check number that is closest to your situation.)	At 11:00 a.m., what is the approximate staff*/child ratio in this program? (Check number that is closest to your situation.)
(28)1___1 to 2 2___1 to 3-4 3___1 to 5-6 4___1 to 7-8 5___1 to 9-10 6___1 to 11-15 7___1 to 16 or more	1___1 to 2 2___1 to 3-4 3___1 to 5-6 4___1 to 7-8 5___1 to 9-10 (47) 6___1 to 11-15 7___1 to 16 or more	1___1 to 2 2___1 to 3-4 3___1 to 5-6 4___1 to 7-8 5___1 to 9-10 (66) 6___1 to 11-15 7___1 to 16 or more
*working directly with children	*working directly with children	*working directly with children

CARE FOR CHILDREN BEFORE AND AFTER SCHOOL

9. Do you have a program providing before or after school care for school age children?

(67) 1___No (If "no," go to question #12) 2___Yes

If "Yes," what age groups are served by this program?

(68-72) ___kindergarten
___grades 1-3
___grades 4-6
___grades 7-8
___other________________________
please describe

ID# (1-8)
CD# '2' = (9)

10. When do you offer services for school age children?
(Check ALL that apply)

(10) ___daily (11)___school holidays (12) ___summer (13)___other________________
please specify

11. How many children do you care for in your before/after school program? _______number (14-16)

CARE FOR CHILDREN WITH SPECIAL NEEDS

12. May children with special needs participate in your program?

(17) 1___Yes 2___No (If "no," please go to #17) 3___Sometimes, depending upon needs

If "Yes" or "Sometimes," what types of special needs are you prepared to handle?

1___mental 2___physical 3___emotional 4___sensory 5___abused children 6___other________________
(please specify)

13. Are special needs children cared for in separate classrooms or integrated into programs with other children?

1___separate classrooms 2___integrated for some activities 3___integrated for all activities

14. At what hour does your program for children with special needs open? ___:___ (20-22)

At what hour does it close? ___:___ (23-25)

15. What is the maximum number of special needs children you can enroll?

(26-28) __________number

16. Do you need a special permit from the state to care for special needs children?

1___No 2___Yes 3___I don't know

17. Which of your programs are licensed?

1___None 2___Infant 3___Toddler 4___Pre-school 5___Before/After School

18. If any of these programs are licensed, by whom?

1___state 2___county 3___city

19. What is the TOTAL number of children currently enrolled in ALL OF THE ABOVE CHILD CARE PROGRAMS (Infant, Toddler, Pre-School, Before/After School, Special Needs) that you operate?

________number (32-34)

MOTHER'S PROGRAM

20. Do you operate a mother's program?

(35) Yes___1 No___2 If no, go to question #25.

If yes, what kind of program is it? (Check ALL that apply)

(36) ___mother's morning out
___parent education
___co-op nursery school or playgroup
(39) ___other

21. How often does it meet? (40) 1___once a week 2___once a month 3___other____________

22. Who may attend? (Check ALL that apply)

(41)___members of congregation
___any mother in the community
___by invitation
(44)___other

23. Are children cared for separately from mothers during the program? (45) 1___yes 2___No

24. How many mothers attend each program? (46-47)_______(approximate)

SECTION II: PROGRAM OPERATION

The questions in this section (25-27) will help us to understand the purposes and goals of your program as well as helping us understand the range of services that you provide.

25. Listed below are a variety of reasons for providing child day care services. Most programs encompass all of these purposes to some extent but place greater emphasis on some more than others. From the list below, please check the THREE purposes (and only THREE for each age group) which best describes your program's approach.

	INFANT	TODDLER	PRE-SCHOOL	BEFORE/ AFTER SCHOOL
a. to encourage children's spiritual development	(48)___	(59)___	(10)___	(21)___
b. to encourage children's appreciation of their family values and culture	___	___	___	___
c. to provide an atmosphere of love, warmth, and understanding	___	___	___	___
d. to meet children's basic needs in a safe and happy environment so that parents can be free for work or other activities	___	___	___	___
e. to help children be obedient, to accept discipline, to improve manners and be accepting of adult supervision and control	___	___	___	___
f. to provide activities in reading and number concepts to prepare children for elementary school	___	___	___	___
g. to assist each child as an individual to be independent, self-reliant	___	___	___	___
h. to learn at his/her own pace and to feel important or special	___	___	___	___
i. to assist children in groups to share, to cooperate with each other and to interact with staff	___	___	___	___
j. to enable children to master cognitive skills appropriate to their age group	___	___	___	___
k. other________________________ (please specify)	(58)___	(69)___	(20)___	(31)___

ID# = (1-8)
CD# '3' = (9)

26. Are parents of children in your program involved in any of the following ways? (Check ALL that apply)

(32)___working with the teacher or other staff on a regular basis
___assisting with field trips
___attending parent-teacher meetings
___providing occasional snacks
___serving on the center's Board
___attending meetings (social, funding, etc.)
(38)___other______________________________ (Describe)

27. Does your program provide any of the following services? (Check ALL that apply.)

(39) ___information and referral for child day care (other than your own program)
___family day care (group child care in private homes)
___parental counseling
___parenting courses
___health care:
___immunizations
___on-site check-ups, treatment
___trips to the doctor, clinic
___dental care
___information about other parent or childrens programs
___sick child care
___emergency drop-off care
(51) ___evening care (after 6 p.m.)

SECTION III: ADMINISTRATION AND FINANCE

Very little is known about the costs of child care, the salary and qualifications of child care workers or about the sources of funding for child care. In answering the questions in this section (28-39) please round all figures to the nearest dollar, estimating where necessary. Leave blank any questions which do not apply to your center.

28. What is the total amount of your annual budget? $__________ (52-57)

29. What is the fee charged to parents per child per week?

ID# = (1-8)
CD# '4' = (9)

(58-60)$______ Infant (61-63) $______ Toddler (64-66)$________ Pre-School (67-69)$______________ before-after school (70-72)$__________ special needs

30. Do parents pay a fixed fee or on a sliding scale per week?

(10) 1_______fixed fee 2_______sliding scale

If a sliding scale is used, what is the range of the scale? $_________ (11-13) to $__________ (14-16)

31. If parents cannot afford the full cost of care, do you offer scholarships/subsidies?

(17) 1___Yes 2___No

If "Yes," what are the sources of funding for scholarships/subsidies? (CHECK ALL THAT APPLY)

(18) ___church support
___local fund-raising
___private, voluntary contributions
___business or industry
___local government
___county government
___state government
___federal government
(26) ___other____ please specify

32. a. Is your child care program incorporated? (27) 1___yes 2___No
If yes, in which of the following ways:

(28) 1___under church incorporation 2___private, not-for-profit 3___under the incorporation of an umbrella agency (YMCA, United Way, Settlement house, etc.)

b. Is your child day care program a proprietorship (owner-operated, for profit)
1___Yes 2___No

33. How are the following aspects of your program funded? Check one response for each category.

		Donated by Church	Partially Paid by Center	Fully Paid by Center
a.	space (indoors, rooms)	(30)1_____	2_____	3_____
b.	space (outdoors, for play, parking)	1_____	2_____	3_____
c.	utilities	1_____	2_____	3_____
d.	equipment repair/replacement	1_____	2_____	3_____
e.	building repair/refurbishing	1_____	2_____	3_____
f.	janitorial services	1_____	2_____	3_____
g.	transportation	(36)1_____	2_____	3_____

34. If space is leased or rented from the church, what is the rental fee per month? __________per month (37-39)

35. Please check below in the appropriate columns whether, in the year 1981, you received funds from any of the sources listed, as well as whether you expect to receive funds from these sources in 1983. Check ALL that are applicable.

	Received in 1981	Expect to receive in 1983
a. Parents' fees	(40) ____	(52) ____
b. Title XX (state social services)	____	____
c. Title IV A(AFDC-welfare-working parents)	____	____
d. Child Care Food Programs	____	____
e. CETA	____	____
f. Other government funds:		
Federal	____	____
State	____	____
Local	____	____
g. Church or religious organizations	____	____
h. Private, voluntary groups (United Way, foundations, etc.)	____	____
i. Business or industry	____	____
j. Individual contributions	(51) ____	(63) ____

36. Please check below in the appropriate column the qualifications that best describe each of the types of staff y may have working in your program:

ID# = (1-8)
CD# '5'=(9)

EDUCATIONAL QUALIFICATIONS (Check highest attained degree)	Director	Teachers	Assistants to Teachers
a. graduate degree (any field)	(10)____	(19)____	(28) ____
b. college degree (major in Early Childhood Education or Child Development)	____	____	____
c. college degree (any field)	____	____	____
d. high school diploma or equivalent	____	____	____
OTHER QUALIFICATIONS (Check ALL that apply.)			
e. some college work in early childhood education, child development	____	____	____
f. some workshops, seminars, courses in child development, early childhood education, child psychology	____	____	____
g. previous child care experience	____	____	____
h. Child Development Associate	____	____	____
i. other ____________ (specify)	(18)____	(27)____	(36)____

37. How many staff are employed by your program?

	Director(s)	Teachers	Assistants to Teachers	Others (cooks, drivers, maintenance)
Full-time:	(37-38) ____ (number)	(39-40) ____ (number)	(41-42) ____ (number)	(43-44) ____ (number)
Part-time:	(45-46) ____ (number)	(47-48) ____ (number)	(49-50) ____ (number)	51-52) ____ (number)

38. What is the range of wages paid by your program to staff per month?

ID# (1-8)
CD# '6' =(9)

	DIRECTOR		TEACHERS		ASSISTANTS TO TEACHERS	
wage range (full-time)	$____ (53-57)	to $____ (58-62)	$____ (63-67)	to $____ (68-72)	$____ (10-14)	to $____ (15-19)
wage range (part-time)	$____ (20-24)	to $____ (25-29)	$____ (30-34)	to $____ (35-39)	$____ (40-44)	to $____ (45-49)

39. Do you offer any fringe benefits to your staff in addition to salary?

(50)1___Yes 2___No If Yes, specify______________________

SECTION IV: COMMUNITY AND PARENT INFORMATION

The questions in this section (40-48) will help us to understand something about your community and the parents of the children served by your program.

40. In what kind of community is your program located? (CHECK THE ONE THAT BEST FITS YOUR COMMUNITY)

(51)1___central core of a major metropolitan area
2___fringe of a major metropolitan area.
3___suburb of major metropolitan area: e.g. large lots, open spaces
4___small city (population 10-50,000)
5___small town or village (population under 10,000)
6___rural farming community
7___rural non-farming

41. Do you have any eligibility requirements for admittance to your program?

(52) 1___Yes   2___No (If "No," go to question #43)

If "Yes," which of the following criteria are used to determine eligibility? (Check ALL that apply.)

(53)___age
___income of family
___membership in the church where your center is located
___residence in a specific geographical area
(57)___other___________________ please describe

42. If family income is used in determining eligibility, what is the maximum income (before taxes) allowable?
$_________per year (58-62)

43. Has your program been involved in presenting day care issues and concerns to community groups, legislators, etc?

(63)1___Yes   2___No

44. Are you familiar with any of the following organizations? (Check ALL that apply.)

(64)___Child Welfare League of America
___Children's Defense Fund
___Day Care Council of America
___Four C's
(68)___local child care resource and referral groups
(69)___local child advocacy and/or day care groups
___National Association for the Education of Young Children (or your state affiliate)
___National Black Child Development Institute
(72)___other___________________ specify

45. Has your center been involved in working to improve licensing requirements for day care centers in your community?

ID# (1-8)
CD# '7' = (9)

(10)1___Yes   2___No

46. Family income information - Below please indicate your estimate of the income of the families of children in your child care programs in Column #1. In Column #2 please indicate your estimate of the income of families attending the church where your child care program is housed.

Family Income Levels per year	Column 1 Families of children in your program	Column 2 Families in the church congregation
under $7,000	(11) 1___	(12) 1___
$7,000 - 10,000	2___	2___
$10,000 - 20,000	3___	3___
$20,000 - 30,000	4___	4___
$30,000 - 50,000	5___	5___
above $50,000	6___	6___

47 Indicate the approximate percentage of each racial group participating in the child care program(s) (Column 1) and in the church congregation (Column 2). (Totals for each column should equal 100%.)

Racial/Ethnic Group	Column 1 Children in child care program	Column 2 church members
White (not hispanic)	(13-14)___	(23-24)___
Black (not hispanic)	___	___
Hispanic	___	___
Asian/Pacific Islands	___	___
Native Americans (American Indians, Eskimos, etc.)	(21-22)___	(31-32) ___

48. Indicate the primary and secondary language(s) spoken by:

	Child care program	Congregational members
	(33)______ (primary)	(35)______ (primary)
	(34)______ (secondary)	(36)______ (secondary)

SECTION V: RELATIONSHIP BETWEEN CHILD CARE CENTER AND CHURCH/CONGREGATION

We are especially interested in understanding the nature of the relationship between the child care program and the congregation of the church in which the child care program is located. Questions 49-56 will help us understand the ways in which the relationship can be improved and strengthened.

49. Who sets administrative and financial policy for your program? (Check ALL that apply)

(37-41)___Director ___Board of Directors ___parents board ___church boards ___other___________ please specify

50. If your program is church-sponsored: Do you offer worship experiences (e.g., Bible Stories, etc.) for the children? (42) 1___Yes ___No

51. Are an individual's religious beliefs an important factor in your staff selection?

1___very important 2___somewhat important 3___of little importance 4___not at all important

52. Do you use volunteer services from community groups? (44) 1___Yes 2___No

If "yes," what types of groups provide the volunteers to your program: (Check ALL that apply.)

(45) ___senior citizens programs (RSVP, Foster Grandparents, etc.)
___arts groups (music, drama, etc.)
___employment training program
___coalition of non-profit service agencies
___community service groups
___individuals
___students from local high schools or colleges
(52) ___other___________________ (please describe)

53. Are any services of church staff and/or members of the congregation provided without cost to your program? (Check ALL that are provided)

(53) ___clergy services
___church secretarial services
___consultation by church educational staff
___volunteer time from church members
___donation of supplies
___donation of training materials
(59) ___other___________________

54. Does your program make any financial contributions to the church in which it is located aside from any costs for space and/or other services noted above?

1___Yes 2___No

55. What is the size of the congregation in which your program is housed?

(61) 1___100 members or less
2___101-200 members
3___201-300 members
4___301-500 members
5___501-800 members
6___801-1200 members
7___1201-1600 members
8___over 1600 members

56. In your view, how supportive of your program is the church/congregation in which you are housed? (Circle ONE number)

very supportive — neutral — very unsupportive

(62) 1----------2----------3----------4----------5

(Continued on next page)

SECTION VI - DISCUSSION QUESTIONS (57-60)

57. What is the most serious problem you face in providing child day care?
(63-64)
(65-66)

58. What is the greatest strength of your program? What are you doing most effectively?
(67-68)
(69-70)

59. Do you expect recent federal and state budget cuts to affect your program? If so, describe the impact of these cuts and how you plan to respond to them.
(71-72)
(73-74)

ID# = (1-8)
CD# '8' = (9)

60. Would you like to be part of a network of church day care providers?

(10) 1___Yes 2___No 3___Not sure

If "Yes," what would you like the network to do? (Check ALL that apply)

(11) ___raise consciousness of church re: church related child day care
___share information on program resources
___provide staff training resources
___provide legislative information
___co-ordinate advocacy efforts
___share fund-raising ideas
(17) ___other____________________
(please specify)

Please feel free to attach additional sheets if you wish to provide us with additional information. We are very grateful to you for taking the time to complete this questionnaire. It is our great hope that together we can do much to advance the cause of child day care. We will, of course, share with you our findings.

With every good wish,
Staff of the Child Day Care Project

Appendix 3
Findings: Church-Operated Versus Independently Operated Centers

Results of Analyses Comparing Church-Operated Centers (N = 753) with Independently Operated Centers (N = 589) Within the Sample of Church-Housed Centers Responding to the Follow-up Survey

Question/Variable	Church-Operated Centers (Number)		Independently Operated Centers (Number)
1. Is church membership required for program admittance?	(753)		(589)
yes	1.7%		0.7%
no	98.3%		99.3%
2. Are any families receiving public assistance?	(753)	****	(589)
yes	26.2%		41.1%
no	73.8%		58.9%
3. Ethnic composition of children enrolled—mean %:[a]	(587)		(465)
a. White (not Hispanic)	86.4%		83.7%
b. Black (not Hispanic)	6.7%	*	9.9%
c. Hispanic	4.1%		3.5%
d. Asian	2.6%		2.6%
e. Native American	0.2%		0.3%
4. Type of community served:	(724)	****	(552)
central core of major city	13.4%		9.1%
fringe of major city	18.1%		12.5%
suburb of major city	27.6%		22.5%
small city (10,000–50,000)	24.4%		25.0%
small town or village	13.8%		22.5%
rural farming community	1.5%		7.1%
rural non-farm community	1.1%		1.4%
5. Mean number of children enrolled:			
a. Infant programs—(N)	(181)		(147)
mean	17.2		13.1
b. Toddler programs—(N)	(301)		(248)
mean	20.0	*	16.3
c. Preschool programs—(N)	(731)		(536)
mean	49.8	****	39.4
d. Centers—(N)	(741)		(568)
mean	61.4	****	47.7

[a] Student's t tests were performed on mean %'s within each ethnic category.

*$p < .05$
**$p < .01$
***$p < .001$
****$p < .0001$

Question/Variable	Church-Operated Centers (Number)		Independently Operated Centers (Number)
6. The percent of centers offering each type of program:	(753)		(589)
a. Infant program (birth to 2 yr)	26.2%		27.4%
b. Toddler program (1½ to 3 yr)	43.3%		46.4%
c. Preschool program (3 to 5 yr)	98.5%	****	94.6%
d. Before/after school program	29.4%		31.5%
e. Mother's program	27.1%		27.3%
f. Care of handicapped children	59.9%	**	67.4%
7. Infant programs—time of operation:			
a. Hours per week	(185)		(152)
15 or fewer	18.0%		15.2%
16-29	3.8%		6.0%
30-44	8.2%		7.3%
45 or more	69.9%		71.5%
b. Days per week	(185)		(151)
1-4	27.6%		23.2%
5	71.4%		76.8%
6-7	1.1%		—
c. Months per year	(185)		(152)
1-8	0.5%		2.0%
9-10	22.7%		20.4%
11-12	76.8%		77.6%
8. Toddler program—time of operation:			
a. Hours per week	(307)		(253)
15 or fewer	14.3%		11.1%
16-29	5.5%		5.9%
30-44	8.1%		9.5%
45 or more	72.0%		73.5%
b. Days per week	(308)	*	(256)
1-4	30.2%		21.9%
5	69.5%		78.1%
6-7	0.3%		—
c. Months per year	(308)	*	(257)
1-8	0.6%		1.6%
9-10	30.2%		19.8%
11-12	69.2%		78.6%

*$p < .05$
**$p < .01$
***$p < .001$
****$p < .0001$

Question/Variable	Church-Operated Centers (Number)		Independently Operated Centers (Number)
9. Preschool program—time of operation:			
a. Hours per week	(730)		(545)
15 or fewer	13.4%		11.4%
16-29	5.8%		7.0%
30-44	11.1%		11.9%
45 or more	69.7%		69.7%
b. Days per week	(732)		(546)
1-4	20.9%		22.7%
5	79.0%		77.1%
6-7	0.1%		0.2%
c. Months per year	(739)	***	(548)
1-8	3.5%		5.1%
9-10	56.4%		45.8%
11-12	40.1%		49.1%
10. Special services provided by centers—% offering each service indicated:	(753)		(589)
a. Referral to other day care	49.7%		54.8%
b. Associated family day care	4.8%	*	8.1%
c. Parental counseling	29.6%		30.9%
d. Parenting courses	19.1%		22.1%
e. Routine health care	9.7%	****	20.0%
f. Sick child care	3.1%		3.9%
g. Emergency drop-off care	8.8%	**	13.6%
h. Evening care (after 6:00 p.m.)	0.7%		0.7%
11. Infant program goals (three most important selected):	(169)		(146)
a. Spiritual development	4.7%		3.4%
b. Appreciation of own culture	1.2%		3.4%
c. Provision of love and warmth	92.9%	**	82.2%
d. Basic care to relieve parents	82.8%		80.8%
e. Obedience, manners, discipline	9.5%		6.8%
f. Preparation for school	1.8%		1.4%
g. Independence, self-reliance	21.9%		24.7%
h. Positive self-image	39.6%		35.6%
i. Sharing, cooperation	29.0%		25.3%
j. Normal cognitive development	4.7%	****	20.5%

*$p < .05$
**$p < .01$
***$p < .001$
****$p < .0001$

Question/Variable	Church-Operated Centers (Number)		Independently Operated Centers (Number)
12. Toddler program goals (three most important selected):	(274)		(229)
a. Spiritual development	12.8%	***	4.4%
b. Appreciation of own culture	2.9%		4.4%
c. Provision of love and warmth	81.0%		73.8%
d. Basic care to relieve parents	58.8%		59.4%
e. Obedience, manners, discipline	11.3%		7.4%
f. Preparation for school	3.6%		3.9%
g. Independence, self-reliance	35.0%		39.3%
h. Positive self-image	38.0%		36.7%
i. Sharing, cooperation	40.9%		47.6%
j. Normal cognitive development	11.7%	*	18.8%
13. Preschool program goals (three most important selected):	(650)		(484)
a. Spiritual development	22.2%	****	5.4%
b. Appreciation of own culture	4.6%		3.7%
c. Provision of love and warmth	61.5%	***	50.8%
d. Basic care to relieve parents	26.0%	**	34.1%
e. Obedience, manners, discipline	8.2%		10.7%
f. Preparation for school	18.8%	**	25.2%
g. Independence, self-reliance	38.6%	*	45.2%
h. Positive self-image	43.8%		39.7%
i. Sharing, cooperation	46.3%		51.0%
j. Normal cognitive development	28.3%		31.4%
14. Before/after school program goals (three most important selected):	(191)		(158)
a. Spiritual development	18.8%	**	7.6%
b. Appreciation of own culture	7.3%		8.9%
c. Provision of love and warmth	69.1%	*	56.3%
d. Basic care to relieve parents	66.5%		70.3%
e. Obedience, manners, discipline	16.2%		17.7%
f. Preparation for school	6.8%		8.9%
g. Independence, self-reliance	37.7%		43.7%
h. Positive self-image	26.7%		30.4%
i. Sharing, cooperation	36.1%		36.7%
j. Normal cognitive development	7.9%	**	17.2%

*$p < .05$
**$p < .01$
***$p < .001$
****$p < .0001$

Question/Variable	Church-Operated Centers (Number)		Independently Operated Centers (Number)
15. What is the highest level of education attained by the center's director?	(603)		(423)
postgraduate degree	25.9%		24.6%
college undergraduate degree	60.9%		62.9%
high school diploma/equivalent	13.3%		12.5%
16. What level of educational attainment best describes the center's teachers as a group?	(467)		(351)
postgraduate degree	7.7%		8.5%
college undergraduate degree	68.5%		66.7%
high school diploma/equivalent	23.8%		24.8%
17. What level of educational attainment best describes the center's teacher aides as a group?	(423)		(302)
postgraduate degree	1.4%		0.7%
college undergraduate degree	16.5%		20.5%
high school diploma/equivalent	82.0%		78.8%
18. How important are religious beliefs in staff selection?	(723)	****	(528)
very important	28.2%		5.9%
somewhat important	34.9%		19.5%
of little importance	15.4%		14.0%
not at all important	21.6%		60.6%
19. Do volunteers from community groups help to provide service?	(710)	****	(543)
yes	54.1%		69.6%
no	45.9%		30.4%
20. In what ways do parents help out?	(753)		(589)
a. Work regularly with teacher	21.9%	***	30.2%
b. Help with field trips	79.5%	**	73.2%
c. Provide occasional snacks	71.6%	***	62.1%

*$p < .05$
**$p < .01$
***$p < .001$
****$p < .0001$

Question/Variable	Church-Operated Centers (Number)		Independently Operated Centers (Number)
21. Has the center's director had any education or formal training in early childhood/child development?	(711)		(510)
yes	86.5%		88.0%
no	13.5%		12.0%
22. Have any teachers had education or formal training in early childhood/child development	(714)	*	(520)
yes	90.9%		94.4%
no	9.1%		5.6%
23. Have any teacher aides had education or formal training in early childhood/child development?	(534)	**	(395)
yes	65.7%		75.2%
no	34.3%		24.8%
24. What is the approximate staff/child ratio at 11:00 a.m., considering only staff working directly with children?			
a. Infant programs	(185)	*	(146)
1 adult to 2 children	7.6%		9.6%
1 to 3-4	45.4%		61.0%
1 to 5-6	36.8%		24.7%
1 to 7-8	7.0%		4.8%
1 to 9-10	2.7%		—
1 to 11-15	—		—
1 to 16 or more	0.5%		—
b. Toddler programs	(302)		(248)
1 adult to 2 children	2.6%		3.6%
1 to 3-4	18.5%		27.0%
1 to 5-6	33.4%		37.1%
1 to 7-8	26.5%		20.2%
1 to 9-10	15.9%		10.1%
1 to 11-15	2.3%		1.6%
1 to 16 or more	0.7%		0.4%

*$p < .05$
**$p < .01$
***$p < .001$
****$p < .0001$

Question/Variable	Church-Operated Centers (Number)		Independently Operated Centers (Number)
24. (continued)			
c. Preschool programs	(728)	****	(536)
1 adult to 2 children	1.1%		2.6%
1 to 3-4	3.4%		7.3%
1 to 5-6	14.0%		23.1%
1 to 7-8	34.1%		32.8%
1 to 9-10	28.3%		22.6%
1 to 11-15	17.2%		9.5%
1 to 16 or more	1.9%		2.1%
25. What is the average group or class size?			
a. Infant programs	(172)		(141)
fewer than 6 children	27.9%		30.5%
6-9	37.2%		36.2%
10-18	30.8%		25.5%
19-22	0.6%		2.1%
more than 22	3.5%		5.7%
[mean group size]	[8.51]		[9.21]
b. Toddler programs	(289)	*	(239)
fewer than 6 children	10.0%		15.9%
6-9	30.1%		23.0%
10-18	52.6%		49.8%
19-22	2.4%		5.9%
more than 22	4.8%		5.4%
[mean group size][a]	[11.07]		[11.18]
c. Preschool programs	(627)		(483)
fewer than 6 children	2.7%		4.3%
6-9	12.9%		14.5%
10-18	63.0%		60.0%
19-22	10.7%		10.1%
more than 22	10.7%		11.0%
[mean group size]	[15.32]		[14.88]

[a] The *t* test comparing group means did not reveal a significant difference in central tendency, although the distributions are significantly different by chi-square.

*$p < .05$
**$p < .01$
***$p < .001$
****$p < .0001$

Question/Variable	Church-Operated Centers (Number)		Independently Operated Centers (Number)
26. Is the program operated by the congregation or independently of the congregation under a rental/use agreement?	Not applicable.		
a. Infant programs			
church-operated			
independently operated			
b. Toddler programs			
church-operated			
independently operated			
c. Preschool programs			
church-operated			
independently operated			
d. Child day care centers—all programs under common administration in the same church			
church-operated			
independently operated			
27. Is the program/center a proprietorship—i.e., operated for profit?	(629)	****	(486)
for-profit center	1.6%		21.4%
non-profit center	98.4%		78.6%
28. Is the church board formally involved in setting program policy?	(753)	****	(589)
yes	41.2%		10.2%
no	58.8%		89.8%

*$p < .05$
**$p < .01$
***$p < .001$
****$p < .0001$

	Question/Variable	Church-Operated Centers (Number)		Independently Operated Centers (Number)
29.	Are parents formally involved in setting program policy?	(753)	*	(589)
	yes	52.1%		58.7%
	no	47.9%		41.3%
30.	What is the fee charged to parents per child per week?			
	a. Infant programs	(170)	**	(126)
	no fee	2.9%		5.6%
	$10 or less	17.6%		15.1%
	$11-$25	11.8%		10.3%
	$26-$40	31.2%		23.0%
	$41-$55	27.6%		20.6%
	$56-$85	8.2%		20.6%
	more than $85	0.6%		4.8%
	[mean fee]	[$33.57]	*	[$40.68]
	b. Toddler programs	(282)	**	(211)
	no fee	1.1%		3.3%
	$10 or less	18.8%		15.2%
	$11-$25	13.8%		10.0%
	$26-$40	34.8%		30.3%
	$41-$55	24.1%		23.2%
	$56-$85	5.7%		15.6%
	more than $85	1.8%		2.4%
	[mean fee]	[$33.32]		[$38.55]
	c. Preschool programs	(655)	****	(433)
	no fee	0.6%		4.6%
	$10 or less	26.0%		25.2%
	$11-$25	26.3%		19.9%
	$26-$40	25.3%		23.3%
	$41-$55	16.9%		18.9%
	$56-$85	3.4%		7.4%
	more than $85	1.5%		0.7%
	[mean fee][a]	[$27.38]		[$27.86]

[a] The *t* test comparing group mean did not reveal a significant difference in central tendency, although the distributions are significantly different by chi-square.

*$p < .05$
**$p < .01$
***$p < .001$
****$p < .0001$

Question/Variable	Church-Operated Centers (Number)		Independently Operated Centers (Number)
31. Do parents pay a fixed fee or a sliding scale fee?	(703)	****	(488)
sliding scale fee	6.7%		16.4%
fixed fee	93.3%		83.6%
32. If parents cannot afford the full cost of care, are subsidies or scholarships offered?	(707)	**	(490)
yes	61.5%		53.7%
no	38.5%		46.3%
33. All sources of program funding during 1981:	(693)		(523)
a. Parents' fees	97.8%	****	91.2%
b. Title XX	9.8%	****	22.6%
c. Title IV A	5.8%	****	12.4%
d. Child Care Food Programs	16.3%	****	33.1%
e. CETA	4.9%	****	15.5%
f. Other federal government	3.3%	****	12.4%
g. Other state government	3.5%	****	11.5%
h. Other local government	10.1%		9.9%
i. Church or religious groups	21.4%		18.7%
j. Private voluntary groups	4.5%	****	19.9%
k. Business/industry	2.7%	***	7.6%
l. Individual contributions	33.8%		34.4%
34. Reliance on private versus public funding for programs during 1981:	(693)	****	(523)
private funding only	71.6%		53.7%
private and public funding	27.6%		41.9%
public funding only	0.9%		4.4%
35. Average monthly wages paid to full-time staff:			
a. Director's monthly wage (mean)	Too few cases.		
b. Teacher's monthly wage (mean)			
c. Aide's monthly wage (mean)			

*$p < .05$
**$p < .01$
***$p < .001$
****$p < .0001$

	Question/Variable	Church-Operated Centers (Number)		Independently Operated Centers (Number)
36.	Are any fringe benefits offered to staff?	(708)		(506)
	yes	55.5%		59.9%
	no	44.5%		40.1%
37.	What amount of rent is paid to the church each month?	(671)	****	(515)
	none	65.4%		21.2%
	$1-$100	17.4%		27.0%
	$101-$200	4.2%		13.8%
	$201-$300	3.7%		10.7%
	$301-$500	2.8%		12.0%
	$501-$1,000	3.1%		10.1%
	more than $1,000	3.3%		5.2%
	[mean rent paid]	[$86]	****	[$234]
38.	Degree to which churches subsidize programs:			
	a. Indoor space	(728)	****	(527)
	church donates at no charge	69.8%		29.2%
	church charges below market rate	20.9%		23.0%
	center pays full rent	9.3%		47.8%
	b. Outdoor space	(702)	****	(486)
	church donates at no charge	73.9%		43.4%
	church charges below market rate	18.4%		17.9%
	center pays full rent	7.7%		38.7%
	c. Utilities	(719)	****	(497)
	church provides at no charge	41.0%		28.0%
	church charges less than value	38.9%		34.8%
	center covers entire cost	20.0%		37.2%
	d. Equipment repair/replacement	(706)	****	(511)
	church provides at no charge	10.2%		6.1%
	church charges less than value	23.4%		14.5%
	center covers entire cost	66.4%		79.5%

*$p < .05$
**$p < .01$
***$p < .001$
****$p < .0001$

Question/Variable	Church-Operated Centers (Number)		Independently Operated Centers (Number)
38. (continued)			
e. Building repair	(700)	****	(490)
church provides at no charge	45.1%		39.6%
church charges less than value	41.1%		32.0%
center covers entire cost	13.7%		28.4%
f. Janitorial services	(713)	****	(506)
church provides at no charge	36.9%		24.3%
church charges less than value	30.4%		22.3%
center covers entire cost	32.7%		53.4%
39. Does church provide scholarships or otherwise specifically subsidize participation by children from lower-income families?	(753)		(589)
yes	35.9%	****	13.4%
no	64.1%		86.6%
40. Does the church provide *any* subsidy for program operation or family participation?	(753)	****	(514)
yes	98.1%		87.3%
no	1.9%		12.7%
41. Program director's response to the question, "In your view, how supportive of your program is the church/congregation in which you are housed?":	(717)	****	(550)
very supportive	37.2%		27.5%
supportive	35.1%		27.3%
neutral	19.7%		30.0%
unsupportive	5.9%		9.3%
very unsupportive	2.1%		6.0%

*$p < .05$
**$p < .01$
***$p < .001$
****$p < .0001$

	Question/Variable	Church-Operated Centers (Number)		Independently Operated Centers (Number)
42.	Program director's familiarity with organizations concerned with child care and early education:	(753)		(589)
	a. Child Welfare League of America	14.3%	**	19.9%
	b. Children's Defense Fund	12.6%	**	17.8%
	c. Day Care Council of America	17.0%	****	27.3%
	d. Four C's	15.0%	****	23.9%
	e. Local child care resource and referral groups	55.9%		55.7%
	f. Local child advocacy and/or day care groups	38.0%	*	43.6%
	g. National Association for the Education of Young Children (or state affiliate)	63.2%		62.6%
	h. National Black Child Development Institute	4.0%	*	7.1%

*$p < .05$
**$p < .01$
***$p < .001$
****$p < .0001$

Appendix 4
Findings: For-Profit Versus Non-Profit Centers

Results of Analyses Comparing For-Profit Centers (N = 119) with Non-Profit Centers (N = 1,121) Within the Sample of Church-Housed Centers Responding to the Follow-up Survey

Question/Variable	For-Profit Centers (Number)		Non-Profit Centers (Number)
1. Is church membership required for program admittance?	(119)		(1,121)
yes	—		1.5%
no	100.0%		98.5%
2. Are any families receiving public assistance?	(119)	****	(1,121)
yes	16.0%		35.8%
no	84.0%		64.2%
3. Ethnic composition of children enrolled (mean %):[a]	(90)		(899)
White (not Hispanic)	92.6%	**	84.1%
Black (not Hispanic)	4.0%	*	8.9%
Hispanic	1.5%	*	3.9%
Asian	1.8%		2.8%
Native American	0.2%		0.3%
4. Type of community served:	(115)	****	(1,077)
central core of major city	5.2%		12.8%
fringe of major city	8.7%		16.5%
suburb of major city	27.8%		23.8%
small city (10,000-50,000)	18.3%		26.6%
small town or village	26.1%		16.1%
rural farming community	10.4%		3.2%
rural non-farm community	3.5%		1.0%
5. Mean number of children enrolled:			
a. Infant programs—(N)	(24)		(312)
mean	7.7	*	12.9
b. Toddler programs—(N)	(40)		(504)
mean	12.4		17.9
c. Preschool programs—(N)	(112)		(1,050)
mean	36.2	*	45.2
d. Centers—(N)	(116)		(1,092)
mean	40.8	***	55.5

[a] Students t tests were performed on mean %'s within each ethnic category.

*$p < .05$
**$p < .01$
***$p < .001$
****$p < .0001$

Question/Variable	For-Profit Centers (Number)		Non-Profit Centers (Number)
6. The percent of centers offering each type of program:	(119)		(1,121)
a. Infant program (birth to 2 yr)	21.7%	*	30.9%
b. Toddler program (1½ to 3 yr)	37.7%	*	49.1%
c. Preschool program (3 to 5 yr)	100.0%	*	95.9%
d. Before/after school program	66.7%		69.2%
e. Mother's program	19.1%	*	29.5%
f. Care of handicapped children	62.2%		64.3%
7. Infant programs—time of operation:			
a. Hours per week	(25)		(324)
15 or fewer	8.0%		21.9%
16-29	—		6.5%
30-44	4.0%		9.9%
45 or more	88.0%		61.7%
b. Days per week	(25)	*	(327)
1-4	8.0%		33.6%
5	92.0%		65.4%
6-7	—		0.9%
c. Months per year	(25)		(328)
1-8	—		1.2%
9-10	12.0%		24.9%
11-12	88.0%		73.9%
8. Toddler program—time of operation:			
a. Hours per week	(43)	*	(525)
15 or fewer	11.6%		15.8%
16-29	—		6.6%
30-44	2.3%		11.0%
45 or more	86.0%		66.6%
b. Days per week	(43)		(522)
1-4	14.0%		30.8%
5	86.0%		68.8%
6-7	—		0.4%
c. Months per year	(43)		(524)
1-8	2.3%		1.0%
9-10	16.3%		26.7%
11-12	81.4%		72.3%

*$p < .05$
**$p < .01$
***$p < .001$
****$p < .0001$

Question/Variable	For-Profit Centers (Number)		Non-Profit Centers (Number)
9. Preschool program—time of operation:			
a. Hours per week	(119)		(1,057)
15 or fewer	10.1%		13.7%
16-29	4.2%		6.2%
30-44	13.4%		11.3%
45 or more	72.3%		68.8%
b. Days per week	(119)		(1,060)
1-4	24.4%		22.5%
5	75.6%		77.3%
6-7	—		0.2%
c. Months per year	(119)	*	(1,069)
1-8	6.7%		2.9%
9-10	54.6%		49.6%
11-12	38.7%		47.5%
10. Special services provided by centers—% offering each service indicated:	(119)		(1,121)
a. Referral to other day care	47.9%		54.2%
b. Associated family day care	5.9%		6.7%
c. Parental counseling	26.9%		31.2%
d. Parenting courses	14.3%		20.6%
e. Routine health care	12.6%		14.8%
f. Sick child care	5.0%		3.5%
g. Emergency drop-off care	18.5%	*	11.4%
h. Evening care (after 6:00 p.m.)	—		0.8%
11. Infant program goals (three most important selected):	(22)		(303)
a. Spiritual development	4.5%		7.3%
b. Appreciation of own culture	4.5%		1.3%
c. Provision of love and warmth	81.8%		85.8%
d. Basic care to relieve parents	95.5%		80.9%
e. Obedience, manners, discipline	31.8%	****	6.9%
f. Preparation for school	—		2.3%
g. Independence, self-reliance	13.6%		24.8%
h. Positive self-image	13.6%	*	35.6%
i. Sharing, cooperation	18.2%		32.7%
j. Normal cognitive development	22.7%	*	9.2%

*$p < .05$
**$p < .01$
***$p < .001$
****$p < .0001$

Question/Variable	For-Profit Centers (Number)		Non-Profit Centers (Number)
12. Toddler program goals (three most important selected):	(39)		(466)
a. Spiritual development	10.3%		10.7%
b. Appreciation of own culture	2.6%		3.4%
c. Provision of love and warmth	76.9%		76.6%
d. Basic care to relieve parents	56.4%		61.2%
e. Obedience, manners, discipline	15.4%		8.4%
f. Preparation for school	7.7%		4.1%
g. Independence, self-reliance	28.2%		36.7%
h. Positive self-image	30.8%		36.3%
i. Sharing, cooperation	43.6%		44.4%
j. Normal cognitive development	17.9%		13.7%
13. Preschool program goals (three most important selected):	(104)		(955)
a. Spiritual development	7.7%	*	17.1%
b. Appreciation of own culture	1.9%		4.6%
c. Provision of love and warmth	42.3%	**	57.7%
d. Basic care to relieve parents	19.2%	**	33.8%
e. Obedience, manners, discipline	17.3%	***	7.7%
f. Preparation for school	39.4%	****	19.2%
g. Independence, self-reliance	43.3%		39.8%
h. Positive self-image	40.4%		42.1%
i. Sharing, cooperation	52.9%		46.6%
j. Normal cognitive development	31.7%		29.0%
14. Before/after school program goals (three most important selected):	(33)		(297)
a. Spiritual development	15.2%		14.5%
b. Appreciation of own culture	12.1%		7.4%
c. Provision of love and warmth	39.4%	**	65.7%
d. Basic care to relieve parents	66.7%		68.7%
e. Obedience, manners, discipline	27.3%		15.2%
f. Preparation for school	15.2%		8.1%
g. Independence, self-reliance	27.3%		40.7%
h. Positive self-image	21.2%		29.0%
i. Sharing, cooperation	30.3%		37.4%
j. Normal cognitive development	31.3%	**	10.8%

*$p < .05$
**$p < .01$
***$p < .001$
****$p < .0001$

	Question/Variable	For-Profit Centers (Number)		Non-Profit Centers (Number)
15.	What is the highest level of education attained by the center's director?	(89)		(879)
	postgraduate degree	13.5%		25.3%
	college undergraduate degree	73.0%		61.1%
	high school diploma/equivalent	13.5%		13.7%
16.	What level of educational attainment best describes the center's teachers as a group?	(74)		(698)
	postgraduate degree	6.8%		6.9%
	college undergraduate degree	68.9%		66.8%
	high school diploma/equivalent	24.3%		26.4%
17.	What level of educational attainment best describes the center's teacher aides as a group?	(66)		(613)
	postgraduate degree	1.5%		1.0%
	college undergraduate degree	24.2%		16.0%
	high school diploma/equivalent	74.2%		83.0%
18.	How important are religious beliefs in staff selection?	(112)	***	(1,067)
	very important	8.9%		19.8%
	somewhat important	20.5%		29.4%
	of little importance	14.3%		14.8%
	not at all important	56.3%		36.0%
19.	Do volunteers from community groups help to provide service?	(110)		(1,074)
	yes	54.5%		61.9%
	no	45.5%		38.1%
20.	In what ways do parents help out?	(119)		(1,121)
	a. Work regularly with teacher	14.3%	**	26.9%
	b. Help with field trips	77.3%		75.1%
	c. Provide occasional snacks	69.7%		66.4%

*$p < .05$
**$p < .01$
***$p < .001$
****$p < .0001$

Question/Variable	For-Profit Centers (Number)	Non-Profit Centers (Number)
21. Has the center's director had any education or formal training in early childhood/child development?	(112)	(1,042)
yes	92.0%	86.9%
no	8.0%	13.1%
22. Have any teachers had education or formal training in early childhood/child development?	(101)	(1,056)
yes	88.1%	91.2%
no	11.9%	8.8%
23. Have any teacher aides had education or formal training in early childhood/child development?	(80)	(780)
yes	70.0%	70.4%
no	30.0%	29.6%
24. What is the approximate staff/child ratio at 11:00 a.m., considering only staff working directly with children?		
a. Infant programs	(24)	(322)
1 adult to 2 children	4.2%	10.6%
1 to 3-4	54.2%	52.5%
1 to 5-6	33.3%	29.8%
1 to 7-8	4.2%	5.3%
1 to 9-10	4.2%	1.9%
1 to 11-15	—	—
1 to 16 or more	—	—
b. Toddler programs	(41)	(515)
1 adult to 2 children	4.9%	3.5%
1 to 3-4	14.6%	22.3%
1 to 5-6	29.3%	35.5%
1 to 7-8	31.7%	22.9%
1 to 9-10	19.5%	12.2%
1 to 11-15	—	2.9%
1 to 16 or more	—	0.6%

*$p < .05$
**$p < .01$
***$p < .001$
****$p < .0001$

Question/Variable	For-Profit Centers (Number)	Non-Profit Centers (Number)
24. (continued)		
c. Preschool programs	(115)	(1,057)
1 adult to 2 children	3.5%	2.0%
1 to 3-4	2.6%	5.5%
1 to 5-6	12.2%	19.8%
1 to 7-8	32.2%	32.5%
1 to 9-10	33.0%	24.7%
1 to 11-15	14.8%	13.4%
1 to 16 or more	1.7%	2.1%
25. What is the average group or class size?		
a. Infant programs	(23)	(302)
fewer than 6 children	43.5%	29.5%
6-9	39.1%	34.8%
10-18	17.4%	30.5%
19-22	—	1.0%
more than 22	—	4.3%
[mean group size]	[6.11]	[8.88]
b. Toddler programs	(37)	(488)
fewer than 6 children	21.6%	13.1%
6-9	29.7%	27.7%
10-18	40.5%	51.0%
19-22	8.1%	3.3%
more than 22	—	4.9%
[mean group size]	[9.70]	[10.99]
c. Preschool programs	(99)	(928)
fewer than 6 children	8.1%	3.2%
6-9	16.2%	14.0%
10-18	54.5%	61.9%
19-22	12.1%	10.5%
more than 22	9.1%	10.5%
[mean group size]	[14.35]	[14.98]

*$p < .05$
**$p < .01$
***$p < .001$
****$p < .0001$

Question/Variable	For-Profit Centers (Number)		Non-Profit Centers (Number)
26. Is the program operated by the congregation or independently of the congregation under a rental/use agreement?			
a. Infant programs	(29)	****	(299)
church-operated	17.2%		66.2%
independently operated	82.8%		33.8%
b. Toddler programs	(50)	****	(475)
church-operated	14.0%		60.4%
independently operated	86.0%		39.6%
c. Preschool programs	(102)	****	(951)
church-operated	9.8%		63.2%
independently operated	90.2%		36.8%
d. Child day care centers—all programs under common administration in the same church	(114)	****	(1,001)
church-operated	8.8%		61.8%
independently operated	91.2%		38.2%
27. Is the program/center a proprietorship—i.e., operated for profit?	Not applicable.		
for-profit center			
non-profit center			
28. Is the church board formally involved in setting program policy?	(119)	****	(1,121)
yes	8.4%		30.2%
no	91.6%		69.8%

*$p < .05$
**$p < .01$
***$p < .001$
****$p < .0001$

Question/Variable	For-Profit Centers (Number)		Non-Profit Centers (Number)
29. Are parents formally involved in setting program policy?	(119)	****	(1,121)
yes	10.9%		60.5%
no	89.1%		39.5%
30. What is the fee charged to parents per child per week?			
a. Infant programs	(23)	**	(295)
no fee	4.3%		4.7%
$10 or less	—		23.1%
$11-$25	4.3%		11.9%
$26-$40	34.8%		25.1%
$41-$55	21.7%		22.0%
$56-$85	34.8%		10.5%
more than $85	—		2.7%
[mean fee]	[$45.44]	*	[$33.25]
b. Toddler programs	(41)		(461)
no fee	2.4%		2.8%
$10 or less	4.9%		21.3%
$11-$25	9.8%		12.4%
$26-$40	31.7%		30.8%
$41-$55	31.7%		22.1%
$56-$85	17.1%		8.7%
more than $85	2.4%		2.0%
[mean fee]	[$40.83]		[$33.56]
c. Preschool programs	(102)		(921)
no fee	1.0%		2.4%
$10 or less	30.4%		25.4%
$11-$25	21.6%		23.3%
$26-$40	19.6%		25.6%
$41-$55	21.6%		17.5%
$56-$85	5.9%		4.5%
more than $85	—		1.3%
[mean fee]	[$26.78]		[$27.59]

*$p < .05$
**$p < .01$
***$p < .001$
****$p < .0001$

Question/Variable	For-Profit Centers (Number)		Non-Profit Centers (Number)
31. Do parents pay a fixed fee or a sliding scale fee?	(112)	**	(1,020)
sliding scale fee	3.6%		12.7%
fixed fee	96.4%		87.3%
32. If parents cannot afford the cost of care, are subsidies or scholarships offered?	(105)	****	(1,036)
yes	31.4%		61.1%
no	68.6%		38.9%
33. All sources of program funding during 1981:	(98)		(1,046)
a. Parents' fees	94.9%		94.6%
b. Title XX	8.2%	*	16.5%
c. Title IV A	6.1%		9.4%
d. Child Care Food Programs	20.%	****	26.0%
e. CETA	2.0%	**	10.7%
f. Other federal government	2.0%	*	7.9%
g. Other state government	3.1%		8.2%
h. Other local government	5.1%		10.9%
i. Church or religious groups	4.1%	****	24.4%
j. Private voluntary groups	1.0%		5.5%
k. Business/industry	9.2%	****	38.0%
l. Individual contributions			
34. Reliance on private versus public funding for programs during 1981:	(98)		(1,046)
private funding only	80.6%		61.7%
private and public funding	17.3%		36.4%
public funding only	2.0%		1.9%
35. Average monthly wages paid to full-time staff:			
a. Director's monthly wage (mean)	Too few cases.		
b. Teacher's monthly wage (mean)			
c. Aide's monthly wage (mean)			

*$p < .05$
**$p < .01$
***$p < .001$
****$p < .0001$

Question/Variable	For-Profit Centers (Number)		Non-Profit Centers (Number)
36. Are any fringe benefits offered to staff?	(101)	****	(1,046)
yes	37.6%		59.3%
no	62.4%		40.7%
37. What amount of rent is paid to the church each month?	(112)	****	(1,012)
none	7.1%		52.0%
$1-$100	39.3%		18.6%
$101-$200	15.2%		7.7%
$201-$300	8.9%		6.8%
$301-$500	17.0%		5.4%
$501-$1,000	8.9%		5.3%
more than $1,000	3.6%		4.2%
[mean rent paid]	[$232]	***	[$136]
38. Degree to which churches subsidize programs:			
a. Indoor space	(109)	****	(1,082)
church donates at no charge	10.1%		57.9%
church charges below market rate	18.3%		21.5%
center pays full rent	71.6%		20.5%
b. Outdoor space	(99)	****	(1,032)
church donates at no charge	24.2%		65.9%
church charges below market rate	15.2%		18.1%
center pays full rent	60.6%		16.0%
c. Utilities	(100)	****	(1,053)
church provides at no charge	28.0%		37.7%
church charges less than value	22.0%		37.6%
center covers entire cost	50.0%		24.7%
d. Equipment repair/replacement	(105)		(1,053)
church provides at no charge	4.8%		9.7%
church charges less than value	14.3%		20.2%
center covers entire cost	81.0%		70.1%

*$p < .05$
**$p < .01$
***$p < .001$
****$p < .0001$

Question/Variable	For-Profit Centers (Number)		Non-Profit Centers (Number)
38. (continued)			
e. Building repair	(99)	*	(1,032)
church provides at no charge	47.5%		43.2%
church charges less than value	25.3%		37.9%
center covers entire cost	27.3%		18.9%
f. Janitorial services	(101)	**	(1,052)
church provides at no charge	23.8%		32.9%
church charges less than value	20.8%		27.6%
center covers entire cost	55.4%		39.5%
39. Does church provide scholarships or otherwise specifically subsidize participation by children from lower-income families?	(119)	****	(1,121)
yes	5.0%		29.0%
no	95.0%		71.0%
40. Does the church provide *any* subsidy for program operation or family participation?	(119)	****	(1,121)
yes	82.4%		96.9%
no	17.6%		3.1%
41. Program director's response to the question, "In your view, how supportive of your program is the church/congregation in which you are housed?":	(116)	****	(1,073)
very supportive	30.2%		33.6%
supportive	22.4%		33.4%
neutral	31.9%		22.7%
unsupportive	5.2%		7.5%
very unsupportive	10.3%		2.8%

*$p < .05$
**$p < .01$
***$p < .001$
****$p < .0001$

Question/Variable	For-Profit Centers (Number)		Non-Profit Centers (Number)
42. Program director's familiarity with organizations concerned with child care and early education:	(119)		(1,121)
a. Child Welfare League of America	10.9%		18.0%
b. Children's Defense Fund	5.0%	***	16.5%
c. Day Care Council of America	14.3%	*	23.6%
d. Four C's	18.5%		20.2%
e. Local child care resource and referral groups	47.1%	*	57.4%
f. Local child advocacy and/or day care groups	31.1%	*	42.6%
g. National Association for the Education of Young Children (or state affiliate)	56.3%		63.2%
h. National Black Child Development Institute	4.2%		5.5%

*$p < .05$
**$p < .01$
***$p < .001$
****$p < .0001$

Appendix 5
Findings: Part-time Versus Full-time Preschool Programs

Results of Analyses Comparing Part-time (N = 294) with Full-time (N = 1,115) Preschool Programs Within the Sample of Church-Housed Centers Responding to the Follow-up Survey

Question/Variable	Part-time (<30hrs/wk) Preschool Programs (Number)		Full-time (≥30hrs/wk) Preschool Programs (Number)
1. Is church membership required for program admittance?	(294)	****	(1,115)
yes	4.4%		0.8%
no	95.6%		99.2%
2. Are any families receiving public assistance?	(294)	****	(1,115)
yes	16.7%		36.0%
no	83.3%		64.0%
3. Ethnic composition of children enrolled—mean %:[a]	(233)		(870)
White (not Hispanic)	94.7%	****	82.9%
Black (not Hispanic)	2.1%	****	9.7%
Hispanic	1.7%	**	4.2%
Asian	1.3%	*	2.8%
Native American	0.2%		0.3%
4. Type of community served:	(275)	**	(1,070)
central core of major city	6.9%		12.4%
fringe of major city	14.5%		16.7%
suburb of major city	28.0%		23.9%
small city (10,000-50,000)	21.5%		25.6%
small town or village	21.5%		16.8%
rural farming community	6.5%		3.3%
rural non-farm community	1.1%		1.2%
5. Mean number of children enrolled:			
a. Infant programs—(N)			
mean	not applicable		
b. Toddler programs—(N)			
mean	not applicable		
c. Preschool programs—(N)	(284)		(1,091)
mean	38.1	**	45.8
d. Centers—(N)			
mean	not applicable		

[a] Students' t tests were performed on mean %'s within each ethnic category.

*$p < .05$
**$p < .01$
***$p < .001$
****$p < .0001$

Question/Variable	Part-time (<30hrs/wk) Preschool Programs (Number)	Full-time (≥30hrs/wk) Preschool Programs (Number)
6. The percent of centers offering each type of program:		
a. Infant program (birth to 2 yr)		
b. Toddler program (1½ to 3 yr)		
c. Preschool program (3 to 5 yr)	Not applicable.	
d. Before/after school program		
e. Mother's program		
f. Care of handicapped children		
7. Infant programs—time of operation:		
a. Hours per week		
15 or fewer		
16-29		
30-44		
45 or more		
b. Days per week	Not applicable.	
1-4		
5		
6-7		
c. Months per year		
1-8		
9-10		
11-12		
8. Toddler program—time of operation:		
a. Hours per week		
15 or fewer		
16-29		
30-44		
45 or more		
b. Days per week	Not applicable.	
1-4		
5		
6-7		
c. Months per year		
1-8		
9-10		
11-12		

Question/Variable	Part-time (<30hrs/wk) Preschool Programs (Number)		Full-time (≥30hrs/wk) Preschool Programs (Number)
9. Preschool program—time of operation:			
a. Hours per week[a]	(294)		(1,115)
15 or fewer	67.7%		—
16-29	32.3%		—
30-44	—		14.7%
45 or more	—		85.3%
b. Days per week	(294)	****	(1,115)
1-4	58.8%		15.1%
5	41.2%		84.8%
6-7	—		0.2%
c. Months per year	(294)	****	(1,113)
1-8	7.8%		2.9%
9-10	76.9%		44.3%
11-12	15.3%		52.8%
10. Special services provided by centers—offering each service indicated:	(294)		(1,115)
a. Referral to other day care	40.8%	****	54.4%
b. Associated family day care	3.7%	*	7.1%
c. Parental counseling	26.9%		30.0%
d. Parenting courses	22.4%		19.9%
e. Routine health care	10.9%	****	15.2%
f. Sick child care	2.7%		3.8%
g. Emergency drop-off care	6.1%	***	13.0%
h. Evening care (after 6:00 p.m.)	0.7%		0.6%
11. Infant program goals (three most important selected):			
a. Spiritual development			
b. Appreciation of own culture			
c. Provision of love and warmth			
d. Basic care to relieve parents			
e. Obedience, manners, discipline	Not applicable.		
f. Preparation for school			
g. Independence, self-reliance			
h. Positive self-image			
i. Sharing, cooperation			
j. Normal cognitive development			

[a] No test was performed on this variable since it was used to define part-time/full-time programs.

*$p < .05$
**$p < .01$
***$p < .001$
****$p < .0001$

Question/Variable	Part-time (<30hrs/wk) Preschool Programs (Number)		Full-time (≥30hrs/wk) Preschool Programs (Number)
12. Toddler program goals (three most important selected):			
a. Spiritual development			
b. Appreciation of own culture			
c. Provision of love and warmth			
d. Basic care to relieve parents			
e. Obedience, manners, discipline	Not applicable.		
f. Preparation for school			
g. Independence, self-reliance			
h. Positive self-image			
i. Sharing, cooperation			
j. Normal cognitive development			
13. Preschool program goals (three most important selected):	(246)		(983)
a. Spiritual development	15.0%		15.8%
b. Appreciation of own culture	3.7%		4.4%
c. Provision of love and warmth	55.7%		57.5%
d. Basic care to relieve parents	22.4%	***	33.8%
e. Obedience, manners, discipline	8.5%		9.3%
f. Preparation for school	16.3%	*	22.3%
g. Independence, self-reliance	37.8%		40.8%
h. Positive self-image	43.9%		40.8%
i. Sharing, cooperation	65.9%	****	43.9%
j. Normal cognitive development	25.6%		29.7%
14. Before/after school program goals (three most important selected):			
a. Spiritual development			
b. Appreciation of own culture			
c. Provision of love and warmth			
d. Basic care to relieve parents			
e. Obedience, manners, discipline	Not applicable.		
f. Preparation for school			
g. Independence, self-reliance			
h. Positive self-image			
i. Sharing, cooperation			
j. Normal cognitive development			

*$p < .05$
**$p < .01$
***$p < .001$
****$p < .0001$

Question/Variable	Part-time (<30hrs/wk) Preschool Programs (Number)		Full-time (≥30hrs/wk) Preschool Programs (Number)
15. What is the highest level of education attained by the center's director?	(223)		(854)
postgraduate degree	22.0%		25.5%
college undergraduate degree	65.5%		61.2%
high school diploma/equivalent	12.6%		13.2%
16. What level of educational attainment best describes the center's teachers as a group?	(174)		(691)
postgraduate degree	8.0%		7.4%
college undergraduate degree	63.2%		67.6%
high school diploma/equivalent	28.7%		25.0%
17. What level of educational attainment best describes the center's teacher aides as a group?	(131)		(629)
postgraduate degree	0.8%		1.1%
college undergraduate degree	24.4%		16.1%
high school diploma/equivalent	74.8%		82.8%
18. How important are religious beliefs in staff selection?	(270)		(1,053)
very important	19.6%		18.4%
somewhat important	31.1%		29.2%
of little importance	14.4%		14.2%
not at all important	34.8%		38.2%
19. Do volunteers from community groups help to provide service?	(275)	*	(1,053)
yes	54.9%		61.5%
no	45.1%		38.5%
20. In what ways do parents help out?	(294)		(1,115)
a. Work regularly with teacher	35.0%	****	23.1%
b. Help with field trips	74.5%		77.0%
c. Provide occasional snacks	72.1%		67.1%

*$p < .05$
**$p < .01$
***$p < .001$
****$p < .0001$

Question/Variable	Part-time (<30hrs/wk) Preschool Programs (Number)		Full-time (≥30hrs/wk) Preschool Programs (Number)
21. Has the center's director had any education or formal training in early childhood/child development?	(265)		(1,024)
yes	87.5%		86.7%
no	12.5%		13.3%
22. Have any teachers had education or formal training in early childhood/child development?	(259)	**	(1,039)
yes	86.9%		92.1%
no	13.1%		7.9%
23. Have any teacher aides had education or formal training in early childhood/child development?	(167)		(799)
yes	65.9%		69.1%
no	34.1%		30.9%
24. What is the approximate staff/child ratio at 11:00 a.m., considering only staff working directly with children?			
a. Infant programs	Not applicable.		
1 adult to 2 children			
1 to 3-4			
1 to 5-6			
1 to 7-8			
1 to 9-10			
1 to 11-15			
1 to 16 or more			
b. Toddler programs	Not applicable.		
1 adult to 2 children			
1 to 3-4			
1 to 5-6			
1 to 7-8			
1 to 9-10			
1 to 11-15			
1 to 16 or more			

*$p < .05$
**$p < .01$
***$p < .001$
****$p < .0001$

Question/Variable	Part-time (<30hrs/wk) Preschool Programs (Number)		Full-time (≥30hrs/wk) Preschool Programs (Number)
24. (continued)			
c. Preschool programs	(283)	**	(1,095)
1 adult to 2 children	2.8%		1.9%
1 to 3-4	6.4%		5.0%
1 to 5-6	20.8%		18.0%
1 to 7-8	38.2%		31.2%
1 to 9-10	23.0%		26.2%
1 to 11-15	7.8%		15.3%
1 to 16 or more	1.1%		2.4%
25. What is the average group or class size?			
a. Infant programs	Not applicable.		
fewer than 6 children			
6-9			
10-18			
19-22			
more than 22			
[mean group size]			
b. Toddler programs	Not applicable.		
fewer than 6 children			
6-9			
10-18			
19-22			
more than 22			
[mean group size]			
c. Preschool programs	(153)	*	(1,058)
fewer than 6 children	7.8%		3.4%
6-9	18.3%		14.2%
10-18	57.5%		61.2%
19-22	9.2%		10.2%
more than 22	7.2%		11.2%
[mean group size]	[13.70]	*	[15.04]

*$p < .05$
**$p < .01$
***$p < .001$
****$p < .0001$

Question/Variable	Part-time (<30hrs/wk) Preschool Programs (Number)	Full-time (≥30hrs/wk) Preschool Programs (Number)
26. Is the program operated by the congregation or independently of the congregation under a rental/use agreement?		
a. Infant programs	Not applicable.	
church-operated		
independently operated		
b. Toddler programs	Not applicable.	
church-operated		
independently operated		
c. Preschool programs	(235)	(988)
church-operated	58.3%	58.4%
independently operated	41.7%	41.6%
d. Child day care centers—all programs under common administration in the same church	Not applicable.	
church-operated		
independently operated		
27. Is the program/center a proprietorship—i.e., operated for profit?	(228)	(945)
for-profit center	7.5%	10.8%
non-profit center	92.5%	89.2%
28. Is the church board formally involved in setting program policy?	(294)	(1,115)
yes	28.9%	27.5%
no	71.1%	72.5%

*$p < .05$
**$p < .01$
***$p < .001$
****$p < .0001$

Question/Variable	Part-time (<30 hrs/wk) Preschool Programs (Number)		Full-time (≥30 hrs/wk) Preschool Programs (Number)
29. Are parents formally involved in setting program policy?	(294)	*	(1,115)
yes	49.3%		56.0%
no	50.7%		44.0%
30. What is the fee charged to parents per child per week?			
a. Infant programs			
no fee			
$10 or less	Not applicable.		
$11-$25			
$26-$40			
$41-$55			
$56-$85			
more than $85			
[mean fee]			
b. Toddler programs			
no fee			
$10 or less	Not applicable.		
$11-$25			
$26-$40			
$41-$55			
$56-$85			
more than $85			
[mean fee]			
c. Preschool programs	(250)	****	(934)
no fee	8.4%		1.4%
$10 or less	48.0%		20.9%
$11-$25	31.6%		20.9%
$26-$40	7.2%		29.3%
$41-$55	2.8%		20.9%
$56-$85	1.6%		5.4%
more than $85	0.4%		1.3%
[mean fee]	[$13.59]		[$30.40]

*$p < .05$
**$p < .01$
***$p < .001$
****$p < .0001$

Question/Variable	Part-time (<30/hrs/wk) Preschool Programs (Number)		Full-time (≥30hrs/wk) Preschool Programs (Number)
31. Do parents pay a fixed fee or a sliding scale fee?	(238)	****	(1,019)
sliding scale fee	2.1%		12.5%
fixed fee	97.9%		87.5%
32. If parents cannot afford the cost of care, are subsidies or scholarships offered?	(241)		(1,025)
yes	55.2%		57.4%
no	44.8%		42.6%
33. All sources of program funding during 1981:	(258)		(1,016)
a. Parents' fees	89.5%	****	95.8%
b. Title XX	3.5%	****	17.7%
c. Title IV A	1.2%	****	9.9%
d. Child Care Food Programs	4.7%	****	27.3%
e. CETA	3.1%	***	10.4%
f. Other federal government	7.8%		7.1%
g. Other state government	5.4%		7.4%
h. Other local government	8.1%		10.3%
i. Church or religious groups	18.6%		21.3%
j. Private voluntary groups	5.4%	**	11.4%
k. Business/industry	4.3%		5.1%
l. Individual contributions	24.8%	***	35.7%
34. Reliance on private versus public funding for programs during 1981:	(258)	****	(1,016)
private funding only	81.0%		60.5%
private and public funding	14.7%		37.4%
public funding only	4.3%		2.1%
35. Average monthly wages paid to full-time staff:			
a. Director's monthly wage (mean)			
b. Teacher's monthly wage (mean)	Too few cases.		
c. Aide's monthly wage (mean)			

*$p < .05$
**$p < .01$
***$p < .001$
****$p < .0001$

Question/Variable	Part-time (<30hrs/wk) Preschool Programs (Number)		Full-time (≥30hrs/wk) Preschool Programs (Number)
36. Are any fringe benefits offered to staff?	(253)	****	(1,022)
yes	43.9%		59.9%
no	56.1%		40.1%
37. What amount of rent is paid to the church each month?	(260)	****	(994)
none	56.2%		46.1%
$1-$100	22.7%		20.2%
$101-$200	6.5%		8.9%
$201-$300	8.5%		5.9%
$301-$500	1.9%		7.9%
$501-$1,000	3.5%		6.3%
more than $1,000	0.8%		4.6%
[mean rent paid]	[$79]	****	[$160]
38. Degree to which churches subsidize programs:			
a. Indoor space	(271)	**	(1,058)
church donates at no charge	62.7%		52.5%
church charges below market rate	20.7%		20.9%
center pays full rent	16.6%		26.7%
b. Outdoor space	(257)	*	(1,006)
church donates at no charge	69.6%		61.1%
church charges below market rate	16.3%		17.5%
center pays full rent	14.0%		21.4%
c. Utilities	(264)	****	(1,023)
church provides at no charge	56.1%		32.6%
church charges less than value	28.8%		38.2%
center covers entire cost	15.2%		29.1%
d. Equipment repair/replacement	(261)	****	(1,028)
church provides at no charge	19.2%		6.8%
church charges less than value	19.5%		20.0%
center covers entire cost	61.3%		73.2%

*$p < .05$
**$p < .01$
***$p < .001$
****$p < .0001$

Question/Variable	Part-time (<30hrs/wk) Preschool Programs (Number)		Full-time (≥30hrs/wk) Preschool Programs (Number)
38. (continued)			
e. Building repair	(257)	****	(998)
church provides at no charge	59.9%		39.8%
church charges less than value	29.6%		39.0%
center covers entire cost	10.5%		21.2%
f. Janitorial services	(268)	****	(1,021)
church provides at no charge	51.5%		29.0%
church charges less than value	22.8%		27.2%
center covers entire cost	25.7%		43.8%
39. Does church provide scholarships or otherwise specifically subsidize participation by children from lower-income families?	(294)		(1,115)
yes	27.2%		26.1%
no	72.8%		73.9%
40. Does the church provide *any* subsidy for program operation or family participation?	(294)		(1,115)
yes	93.5%		94.4%
no	6.5%		5.6%
41. Program director's response to the question, "In your view, how supportive of your program is the church/congregation in which you are housed?":	(279)		(1,063)
very supportive	36.2%		32.1%
supportive	34.1%		31.6%
neutral	21.5%		24.6%
unsupportive	6.8%		7.3%
very unsupportive	1.4%		4.3%

*$p < .05$
**$p < .01$
***$p < .001$
****$p < .0001$

Question/Variable	Part-time (<30hrs/wk) Preschool Programs (Number)		Full-time (≥30hrs/wk) Preschool Programs (Number)
42. Program director's familiarity with organizations concerned with child care and early education:	(294)		(1,115)
a. Child Welfare League of America	10.5%	**	17.8%
b. Children's Defense Fund	11.6%		15.0%
c. Day Care Council of America	10.5%	****	24.1%
d. Four C's	14.3%	*	19.7%
e. Local child care resource and referral groups	46.3%	***	57.4%
f. Local child advocacy and/or day care groups	32.0%	**	41.9%
g. National Association for the Education of Young Children (or state affiliate)	54.4%	**	63.5%
h. National Black Child Development Institute	1.7%	**	6.1%

*$p < .05$
**$p < .01$
***$p < .001$
****$p < .0001$

A Little Child Shall Lead Us: Observations for Churches

Commentary by Peggy L. Shriver

Associate General Secretary
Office of Research, Evaluation, and Planning
National Council of Churches

That churches are major providers of child care in the United States comes as no real surprise to national church leaders. In their travels around the country, they have come across innumerable churches with various kinds of day care programs. They benefit from this study, however, like stargazers who have looked into the brilliant night sky and have had Orion pointed out to them. They have seen the stars all along but have needed to have the configuration pointed out, and once having seen it, they wonder why it was not visible before.

Before chastising national church executives, who are already prone to self-flagellation, for failing to keep careful records of so large a phenomenon as appears to be documented in this study, we need to remind ourselves that even the pastors were not good sources of information about these programs. More significant indeed is the overwhelming evidence that local churches have a resourcefulness, vitality, and sensitivity that have brought about a plethora of programs and assorted administrative and financial responses. National leaders may rejoice that it is not always necessary for them to be the stimulus to creativity and concern in the local church. With grace, they will surely acknowledge a humbler role for themselves—that of servant connectors of many different experiences and concerns with one another—as the Child Advocacy Working Group within the National Council of Churches is already beginning to discover.

Not all Christians agree that child care outside the traditional home is an acceptable service to the community. Some see day care as preempting the role of mother and therefore undermining a community's expectations that women should be looking out for their own children. Child care programs seem to have come into existence in local churches from a great variety of motivations, however. One must beware of confusing symptoms with cause. Are women bringing children to day care programs simply because the programs exist, or because—again for a variety of reasons—they need a place to care for their children while they work? Do the children themselves, in certain sterile or unhealthy or lonely environments, have a need for one another? The influx of women into the work force has been staggering and has shown no sign of a reversal in recent years. Day care is largely a response to, not the instigator of, that trend.

The motives identified by the study (Christian education, pastoral care, community service, evangelism, stewardship, and social justice) are intermingled in many local churches that house child day care. Perhaps it is these varied motives that have contributed to the inability of pastors and church denominational leaders to see child care clearly as national or local church mission. A program that is begun to bring a little revenue to an under-utilized church building is not perceived primarily as a part of the church's mission. A church that has responded to a social agency request or to a community organization's need for space may not immediately see itself as participating in an act of mission. As programs grow or settle into a church, the motivations may undergo subtle shifts. Leaders change in the child care program; pastors are replaced; church committees become more active and see new opportunities for collaboration and service. Such programs may become closer to a congregation's sense of responsibility and involvement, or they may become increasingly remote and alien to the purposes of the church. It may well be that an important role for national leadership to play is to assist churches in finding ways to reassess their child care programs from time to time, in rediscovering the reasons for these programs as a part of their life.

Differing motivations also quite obviously spawn differing administrative relationships. One is impressed in this study with the imaginative problem-solving and administrative connections that have evolved in many churches. Some relationships are surely more effective than others. The past 20 years or so have brought forth a marvelous variety of "case histories." Work is needed to discover the most successful administrative links between child care programs and local church leadership for achieving the goals appropriate to particular motivations. Such study could be instructive for other kinds of programs that churches may sponsor with varying degrees of involvement and kinds of motivation. Programs like "Meals on Wheels," social events for the elderly, jobs and career assistance, and other attempts to meet human needs with special leadership could learn from an analysis of the child care experience.

Two of the study findings should please Christians who honor generosity and inclusiveness. Churches have apparently been generous landlords not only to their own church-operated programs but also to independents and for-profit programs. Having decided that child care meets various important human needs, they have been doing their part to make it affordable. They have multiplied their "talents," so that even though they may have had little direct funding to offer, they have supplied free or low-rent space, services, and often volunteer help. Furthermore, they have belied the stereotype of simply serving their own congregations' needs with nursery care that is provided for only a few hours of the week. The study shows that 99% of programs have been open to the community, and the predominance of full-day programs demonstrates the firm intention of these child care providers to meet a heavy demand from their environment for help.

Inclusiveness may have been offered at the expense of some other values within the church, however. Spiritual development has not ranked high among the goals of church-housed child care programs, although those that are church-operated rank this goal higher than the independents rank it. A classic dilemma of mission and service within the church is revealed here. Is it possible to provide spiritual enrichment, evangelistic opportunity, and Christian education, along with the service to a community's need for child care, in a manner that does not hold such need hostage to a church's missionary zeal? Does child care provide another version of the "rice Christian"? Conversely, have churches so carefully avoided any tendency to "use" child care for their own outreach purposes that they have neglected some hopes and expectations of participant parents for their children? The answers to these questions will differ from church to church. One might at least hope that churches have been sensitive to counteract negative experiences or images that are innate to such close-quarter living.

Perhaps a future network of child-care-sponsoring churches will explore ways that churches have interpreted their own church programs constructively to children in their child care centers. Have children had a tour of other parts of the church, perhaps hearing the organ play in the sanctuary or learning about the stories in the church stained glass? When there is a funeral or a wedding, is this simply an interruption of children's outdoor play schedule, or is the event given some interpretation by church staff? Are older women in the congregation seen chiefly as people who are annoyed by sandy feet walking through the lounge, or are they seen as people with interesting skills to demonstrate and stories to share? Are children welcomed in some parts of the church on Sunday, but regarded as intruders on Monday? Have members of the congregation discovered the opportunities and needs within the day care center for their special gifts? Have the particular needs of various families for day care, such as those mentioned in the Samaritan programs, opened up other concerns for ministry?

Because any program that becomes identified with a local congregation tends to brighten or tarnish the image of that congregation in a community, a dilemma for many local churches must surely be to wonder how much control they should exert in requiring child care programs, especially independent ones, to meet certain standards of justice and ethics that the church wants to uphold. This may conflict with the autonomy of professionals in child care. A program that is too tightly regimented or too loosely disciplined, one that makes no effort to cross race or class boundaries, one that is sloppy in its care or more anxious to preserve things rather than children—all of these public impressions become to some degree a legacy of the church within the community to which it brings its invitation of the Gospel. In the name of its own integrity as well as that of the program it supports, a church cannot ignore the necessity of some standards and policies. How these are negotiated and which ones are primary could be issues of an important study. This relates to another long-standing issue: When churches are attempting to work in coalitions, when does compromise become compromising?

The varieties of child care programs illustrate the multitude of human needs that can be touched through work with children and families. Not every program can attempt to meet all the kinds of care required within a community. A role for local ecumenical councils, ministerial associations, or other ecumenical clusters may be discovered here. Who knows which churches in a community take children after school; make a special effort to care for the disabled; have extended hours; provide infant care; have a parents' program, a mothers' social gathering, a collaboration with public health preventive programs, or an emphasis upon the arts? An ecumenical agency could gather this information, review needs not being met, find opportunities being missed, share new ideas for using community resources, and assist centers to work with other community agencies. It may also become the place where larger issues within the community are addressed as people become aware of them through work with children.

That is a final point that needs to be stressed. One might think child care is one of the least controversial of programs, for it is difficult to argue with the value of children having loving care, safe surroundings, and opportunities for play and learning. Even those who would prefer to see a child kept at home by the side of a parent find a day care program better than leaving a child alone if a mother must work. But caring for people is not tidy. Churches have discovered that almost any attempt to provide simple help is ultimately *not* simple. In India there is a saying: "If one hunts for ivory, one finds an elephant attached." If one attempts to help an individual, one finds a society attached. This was demonstrated profoundly as our churches began to delve into the problem of world hunger. Feeding hungry mouths led churches to explore why there was no food, or no job to pay for food, or no hope that circumstances would change. It is not unlikely that care for migrant children will lead to questions of justice about the lives of migrants, or that care for children from distraught families will bring serious questions about child abuse, broken homes, unemployment, or welfare policies. This is not an argument to discourage involvement in child care programs by churches. It is rather an invitation to even deeper adventure into the mysteries of human society and what God means by an incarnational love of neighbor as oneself.

A Day Care Perspective on the Study

Commentary by Gwen G. Morgan

Child Care Consultant and Lecturer
Wheelock College

This study gives us an intriguing snapshot, a still picture at a moment in time, of a large and very important part of the overall day care scene. Like our other pictures of child day care, it is blurry in places and hard to make out in detail, but it has a few sharply focused outlines. The snapshot only includes day care in churches that are part of the National Council of Churches, leaving a great deal of other religiously affiliated day care undescribed. It is also a picture only of those day care providers who answered the questionnaire, and they may differ in some ways from those who did not. All of this may limit our ability to draw conclusions about day care outside the frame of the snapshot. Nevertheless, the data from those who participated in the study give us some rich information.

The first and probably the most striking finding of the study is the massive involvement of churches in child day care. This fact alone has many important implications. The study also illuminates the nature of day care in the United States. While the media have tended to view day care, when they have viewed it at all, as either government-run services for the poor or as corporate chains, most day care is private non-profit, or private for-profit but run by small owner-operators. This study finds that a high proportion of this private segment of day care is housed in church space or is run by the churches themselves.

The study also finds that churches have become involved as a response to locally perceived needs in their communities or in their congregations for educational and/or charitable services for children and their families. The very few for-profit programs in churches tend to be idealistic and owner-operated. Furthermore, their host churches are not using day care to defray building expenses but are giving generously of their space to a perceived need.

Like child day care in general, the day care in churches has the twin goals of providing developmental experience for children and needed support for families, particularly for growing numbers of working parents. The spiritual mission of churches makes them deeply aware of the necessity for every child to be welcomed into a caring community that nurtures human growth; churches are natural allies for day care. Their local perception of new needs of families and their responses, particularly the Good Samaritan responses, are very important, and significantly, these responses have preceded ideology. Our society needs further leadership from the churches in articulating what they know—that child day care offers a much-needed community support for today's families.

Like child day care in general, day care in churches is in transition. The old distinction between part-day educational programs and full-day care centers, always tinged with class bias, is still present but is changing with the growing realization that working families are choosing both types of programs as care for their children.

The study found that day care in churches is supported from a variety of sources including local, state, and federal governments and the churches themselves. In massive proportions, day care is already the public-private partnership it has become fashionable to seek. It already includes a high degree of volunteer participation. Dependent for part of its survival on government help for some families, it has been hard-hit by the reduced concern of its governmental partner. The anguished voices of day care providers themselves, included in the report, provide a strong note of reality. Despite the six mission-related reasons for church involvement with child day care— Christian education, pastoral care, evangelism, stewardship, community service, and social justice—day care in churches is no bed of roses, these voices tell us clearly.

The study itself could have a positive effect on the day care field. For example, for the day care now in churches, two kinds of Church help might result from response to the study's findings. The first would be to legitimize child day care as an important and valid part of the mission of the Church. This would help day care providers in their human relations with their host churches. Although the fact of so much day care in churches is a general indication of strong church support, there are common human relations problems reported by individual providers that might be diminished by stronger support from higher levels of the Church.

The second kind of help for day care in churches might be development of more resources to improve quality. The study found some evidence that program quality tends to be slightly lower in church-operated than in independently operated programs. These distinctions in quality are not great, and the study found generally good quality in church-operated day care. Nevertheless, with the depth of understanding the Church as a whole has for the nature of human development, it is unthinkable that it would accept anything less than its best effort on behalf of children in its care. It seems reasonable to hope that the same high quality of resources the Church has brought to its Christian education programs could be developed for its day care programs, either centrally or denominationally. The day care field in general needs more materials and more training, and the church could contribute significantly to meeting those needs. Some of the materials and training might address the spiritual aspect, but much might address child development programming more generally, since most of the day care programs in churches are not narrowly focused on religious education.

Beyond these two obvious responses the study might elicit from the Church, there are ways the study might affect the day care field through influencing churches that are not now operating or hosting day care programs.

The study documents the growing need of working parents for child day care. Churches can take credit for filling much of this need until now, but the need will continue to increase and more church help would make a significant difference. By demonstrating the importance of church day care services to children and their families, the study and its follow-up activities might influence more churches to make space available for child day care. It should be emphasized that a key factor in the founding of many high quality day care centers has been the low-cost space made available by churches.

Those churches without space to share might be stimulated to contribute to scholarship funds to help parents pay for the child care they need in the community. The central problem for day care providers has been the fact that most parents cannot pay the cost of a quality day care program, and the unacceptable solution until now has been to underpay the staff that provide the care. More church interest in this reality, well expressed in this study, might bring more local scholarship funds to enhance parental ability to pay.

Finally, local churches might contribute to the development of more effective delivery systems for child day care in their communities. At present, church-housed providers, like day care providers in general, are rather isolated from one another and from other providers in the community. The need for the 1980s is to create a delivery system that works for parents and providers by linking church-housed providers with one another, with other day care providers, and with other community agencies. There should be resource and referral services for parents; planning for unmet needs; more support from employers and private charities as well as churches; and direction of both public and private funds into programs that do not segregate children by funding source. This delivery system needs to be developed locally, since child day care is very local in nature. Local church leadership could play a significant role, with others in the community, in overcoming resistance to change and creating a better day care system.

From a secular day care perspective, the nature of the Church's response will be extremely important. It is impossible to ignore the

Church's massive participation in child day care, and any initiative by national church agencies will have far-reaching repercussions for the entire day care community.

Vertical ("top-down") responses to child day care needs, either ecumenically or denominationally, can enrich a major part of the day care field through validation of mission, provision of training and other program resources, expansion of provision, and leadership. This welcome enrichment would be a major contribution to the day care of the future.

Exclusively vertical support, however, might reinforce the tendency the study found for church-related day care to be somewhat removed from the secular mainstream. Thus, vertical responses need to be balanced with horizontal responses that involve local parishes and church-housed providers with other providers and agencies in their communities in the development of effective local delivery systems.

Finally, there is the potential, as suggested by the study, for the Church to exercise leadership in addressing critical and timely issues in child care. At present, the growing tendency of the states to exempt churches from licensing standards is one such issue. Those who seek to exempt churches base their arguments on religious grounds. Urgently needed are persons and groups, also of religious persuasion, to support the regulation of child care programs to ensure the well-being of young children. Further, these groups might well join with others in the child care community to improve and reform the regulatory systems in the states. The National Council of the Churches of Christ, U.S.A., has taken one step toward such bold leadership in the present work.